Desire Lines
A Guide to Community Participation in Designing Places

Lesley Malone

RIBA  Publishing

© RIBA Publishing, 2018

Published by RIBA Publishing, 66 Portland Place, London, W1B 1NT

ISBN 978-1-85946-727-5

The right of Lesley Malone to be identified as the Author of this Work has been asserted in accordance with the Copyright, Designs and Patents Act 1988 sections 77 and 78.

British Library Cataloguing-in-Publication Data
A catalogue record for this book is available from the British Library.

Commissioning Editor: Alex White
Project Editor: Daniel Culver
Production: Richard Blackburn
Designed and typeset by BORN
Printed and bound by Page Bros, Norwich, UK
Cover image/Image credits: www.shutterstock.com

While every effort has been made to check the accuracy and quality of the information given in this publication, neither the Author nor the Publisher accept any responsibility for the subsequent use of this information, for any errors or omissions that it may contain, or for any misunderstandings arising from it.

www.ribapublishing.com

BIOGRAPHICAL INFORMATION

Lesley Malone has an MSc in Social Research Methods, specialising in the study of public space and people-centred urban design. With a career background in the built environment in a variety of research, information and communications roles, she is now a freelance writer and consultant.

ACKNOWLEDGEMENTS

Many thanks to everyone who shared their insights and ideas:
Ian Baggott, Alison Bromilow, Charles Campion, Robert Cheesman, Eileen Conn, Vinita Dhume, Kate Digney, Alan Divall, Joanna Ede, Catherine Greig, Kevin Harris, Richard Hayward, Gemma Leigh Holyoak, Rachel Leggett, Paul Mahony, Michelle Male Shaw, Rose Marshall, Perry Miller, Rebekah Paczek, Neil Porter, Mandy Renshaw, Anna Rose, Graham Ross, Jessica Topham and David Wilcox.

Immense gratitude and love to Caroline Jago for her patience and support.

Contents

Desire Lines: A Guide to Community Participation in Designing Places

1   Introduction

'Architecture is too important to be left to architects.'

– Giancarlo De Carlo

1.1   WHAT THIS BOOK IS ABOUT

This book is about people.

It offers guidance to designers on consulting with local communities and enabling their meaningful participation in projects. It starts from the premise that any participation programme can and should be thought of as a research project, and as such should be carried out with a research mindset and methods. So it aims to get designers to think more like researchers and to implement some research basics to improve the quality of community participation.

Greater methodological rigour in participation programmes makes for more people-centred design processes, whatever the scale or nature of the project. It means that approaches to involving local people will be more impartial in their conception, and more thorough in gathering and interpreting information. It also means greater evidence-based design, and more transparent decision-making, authenticity, inclusion and knowledge-building. Most of all, it means the voices that need to be listened to can be heard more clearly. So communities, clients and designers all benefit.

What it covers

Chapter 2 takes a brief tour around some research essentials relating to community participation. This includes aspects such as having clearly defined research objectives from the outset, coupled with an effective strategy for gathering and synthesising information. So this chapter focuses on the three big questions to answer at the start of any research project:

1. What do we need to know?
2. Who can provide the information we need?
3. How shall we gather and analyse this information?

Chapters 3 to 8 offer practical guidance on some information-gathering methods. The chapter order follows the 'Spectrum of Participation' shown in Table 1.1, which characterises levels of public participation within civic decision-making from 'no participation' to 'empowered'. This group of chapters starts with the 'no participation' options of observation and diary studies, via more consultative methods like meetings, exhibitions and surveys, to the other end of the spectrum and collaborative approaches like charrettes, workshops and co-design. Each chapter has roughly the same structure and looks at the types of information each method is suitable for generating, and then preparation, implementation and working with the gathered data. Quick guides to good practice in common aspects of these methods are dotted throughout, covering qualitative data analysis, running public events, communications and reporting on research findings.

TABLE 1.1

The Spectrum of Participation. The International Association of Public Participation devised the Spectrum (IAP2, 2014), which can be applied within many spheres of public life to describe levels of community involvement. The sample activities are specific to spatial design.

<< Less participation -- More participation >>

LEVEL					
NO PARTICIPATION	INFORM	CONSULT	INVOLVE	COLLABORATE	EMPOWER
Sample activities					
Observation, diary studies	Public exhibitions, newsletters, websites	Public meetings, surveys, focus groups, online forums, social media	Workshops, liaison / steering groups	Charrettes, co-design, neighbourhood planning	?
Participation goal					
None	To provide the public with balanced and objective information to assist them in understanding the problem, alternatives, opportunities and/or solutions.	To obtain public feedback on analysis, alternatives and/or decisions.	To work directly with the public throughout the process to ensure that public concerns and aspirations are consistently understood and considered.	To partner with the public in each aspect of the decision, including the development of alternatives and the identification of the preferred solution.	To place final decision-making in the hands of the public.
Promise to the public					
None	You will be kept informed.	You will be kept informed. Your concerns and aspirations will be listened to and acknowledged. There will be feedback on how public input influenced the decision.	You will be kept informed. Your concerns and aspirations will be directly reflected in the alternatives developed. There will be feedback on how public input influenced the decision.	You will provide advice and innovation in formulating solutions. Your advice and recommendations will be incorporated into decisions to the maximum extent possible.	Your decisions will be implemented.

The two final chapters look in more specific ways at the issues involved in working with people.

Chapter 9 discusses ethical and inclusive practice, and how an approach informed by research ethics can strengthen work with communities – especially when marginalised groups, children and young people are involved. The final chapter gives a voice to participants. I interviewed representatives from a range of local groups to discuss their experiences of participation programmes and include excerpts from those discussions. These insights from real-world projects can help create relevant, engaging programmes, and highlight some avoidable pitfalls.

A word about the title. Desire lines are the paths people create through regular usage. There are other names for them: social trails, pirate paths, cow paths, donkey paths, goat tracks, elephant trails, and doubtless more. They appear where people repeatedly choose to walk, and usually signify a route from A to B that is quicker or more easily navigated than the formal path provided (see Figure 1.1 a, b, c). This can be interpreted as a design failure; the formal path was rejected because there was a better way. Or perhaps there's no path at all. Desire lines can show the mismatch between what a designer thinks best and what people actually prefer. They also speak of a sense of local knowledge, where local people see better routes than those by designers or planners. The symbolism seems apt for a book about putting local people at the centre of the design process, and allowing their needs and wishes to shape development.

Who it's for

The book is intended for practitioners who want to develop more people-centred, community-led design approaches. This includes architects, urban designers, landscape architects and other built environment professionals involved in placemaking or public realm planning and design. It will be useful to students in these disciplines, both as guidance on projects involving primary fieldwork and as general preparation for professional practice, where skills in working with local communities are increasingly sought after. Community groups and clients will also find some new ideas for making good use of local expertise and bringing it into the design process.

Figures 1.1a-c: Desire lines

1.2	**WHAT IT OFFERS**

This book addresses three main needs.

Firstly, design training doesn't always equip practitioners with skills in managing consultation or community involvement. Yet placemaking is about people as much as places; at its heart is substantial engagement with communities, and their authentic participation and collaboration. So people-centred design requires people-centred consultation and participation programmes. At the same time, increasing numbers of designers in the built environment are looking to move away from top-down traditions and develop a more socially engaged practice that genuinely responds to local needs and aspirations. However, my perception is that this needs a greater level of rigour in collecting and analysing information. So this book offers practical guidance for practitioners who want to research and support communities more effectively.

Secondly, there are more and more people active in their communities who expect design professionals to treat them as partners in the development process, as comments in Chapter 10 show. Civic societies, heritage groups, community organisations and the like are increasingly knowledgeable. They can be valuable allies and they also know a tick-box exercise when they see one. So designers need to up their game and offer meaningful opportunities for involvement from the outset, to make the most of their knowledge.

Thirdly, streetscapes and public space are vital elements of urban infrastructure, spatially and socially. They can create value in every way. Not only this, but also the streets and spaces people navigate, and the visual and sensory stimuli they experience there have undoubted psycho-social effects, including both immediate and long-term influences on mood, stress levels, interactions and behaviour. There are more profound mental health aspects too. Depression and anxiety are known to correlate with social stress and a sense of alienation and isolation in urban environments. (Evidence shows that monotonous street-level facades and no greenery are the most effective ways to induce these states.) When designers can access knowledge that enables them to design for enjoyment and mental wellbeing, where people feel more positive, more comfortable, healthier, safer and more socially connected, why not use it? And what better way to generate this knowledge and understand people's needs, wants and preferences than through offering them meaningful participation in the planning and design process?

There's no one-size-fits-all solution to consultation or engagement, of course. What works with one community and project may not be appropriate for a similar community or type of project elsewhere. What this book offers is advice on the main ingredients, rather than recipes; how these ingredients are combined, flavoured and served up is for the design team to decide as the project requires. It's also worth noting that research and engagement work should be ongoing, informing the project as it develops from inception to delivery. I emphasise the importance of an early start, but good engagement is integral to a good overall design process and should continue throughout.

1.3	WHY COMMUNITY PARTICIPATION MATTERS

The project benefits

Good research and engagement enable good design. And good design adds value. The art and science of discovering what people like and want has evolved to advanced levels in some design fields, in particular product design and digital usability/user experience (UX) research. In human terms, the research goal is maximum user satisfaction; in commercial terms this means creating value, efficiency and profitability through good design. The approaches used in these fields are discussed in more detail in the next chapter. Suffice to say that an established research cycle is central to the process, whereby users test product prototypes, which are then refined to incorporate their feedback, and re-tested and refined until optimum functionality, usability and aesthetic quality are reached. When built environment projects are driven by much the same requirements, wouldn't the design process benefit from (a) involving users from the start, and (b) adopting a methodical approach to understanding and incorporating their needs and wants?

By providing insight into people's views and preferences, good local participation can also reveal new perspectives and possibilities for a site. A project can only gain from being informed by local knowledge, so why not listen to the experts? Don't start by presenting detailed plans. Involving community groups in the ideation stages increases the likelihood of producing proposals that are acceptable to the wider community, as well as a smooth passage through planning. Good participation can also generate design improvements, making fuller use of the space and improving inclusivity, for instance, and generating greater local support – which again benefits everyone.

Furthermore, genuine community participation can be a valuable learning experience for designers as well, when they're willing to listen, to treat the community as the expert, and to work with local people as partners. Blundell Jones et al. (2005) call for 'transformative participation', emphasising that participation is an opportunity to develop professional expertise, not a threat to it, which should drive designers to discover new ways of working, thinking and communicating.

Figure 1.2

Learning form the High Line	One of the co-founders of the iconic High Line in New York, Robert Hammond, stated that he considered the project to have 'failed' local communities (Bliss, 2017). Specifically, Hammond pointed to the neglect of meaningful engagement with residents and local businesses from the start of the planning and design process, which he considers a grave oversight. The High Line is a phenomenally successful project, attracting millions of visitors every year; a massive commercial hit as well as a design milestone. However, according to Hammond, it has harmed surrounding neighbourhoods by causing rapid gentrification, which has exacerbated economic inequality and priced out small businesses. He now believes that this could have been mitigated or averted by engaging with local communities from the outset, and regrets that opportunities to improve the lot of existing impoverished communities were missed. 'Instead of asking what the design should look like, I wish we'd asked, "What can we do for you?"' Hammond said, 'Because people have bigger problems than design.'

The community benefits

A programme offering authentic participation can yield significant community dividends. Bringing local people together to help develop a project can generate a sense of civic pride, enable new connections and networks, and build confidence, skills and knowledge, which can be especially valuable when marginalised groups get involved. Young people in particular can benefit when they're offered a meaningful role in the process. It can help them feel they're part of the community and have something to offer, and it gives them experience of team-working for the greater good, as well as opportunities to learn new skills. A project aiming to deliver liveability, inclusivity and increased social cohesion cannot be expected to succeed in these aims without bringing communities into decision-making. By the same token, failing to invite local communities to participate can have profound consequences.

People increasingly want and expect to be involved in local decisions that affect them. Many more now feel that their views on changes to their local environment should be heard from the outset, and that it is unacceptable at the 'consultation' stage to be steered towards endorsing decisions that appear to have already been made. Design can influence – for good or ill – people's physical and mental wellbeing, local business prosperity, and an area's economic fortunes. With these significant long-term implications, shouldn't communities have a greater say in what they get? However, people-centred design means engaging with a wide array of socio-economic and cultural groups who use and experience public space in many different ways. So how to create inclusive spaces that meet diverse – and sometimes conflicting – needs and wishes, without privileging one group or excluding another? Only by looking, listening and learning.

Desire Lines: A Guide to Community Participation in Designing Places

2

Research essentials for community participation

'I never think about beauty. I only think about how to solve the problem. But when I have finished, if the solution is not beautiful, I know it is wrong.'

– R. Buckminster Fuller

2.1	INTRODUCTION

This chapter is intended to equip designers with the essential research principles needed for effective community participation. My aim is to get designers to start thinking like researchers, and paying attention to these basics – introduced in this chapter – will go a long way towards that. We look at putting these principles into practice in designing an engagement programme/research project (I'll treat these as synonymous). There are three big questions to ask when planning a programme:

1. What do we need to know?
2. Who can provide the information we need?
3. How shall we gather and analyse this information?

The answers form the basis of the research strategy, which will be a key document guiding the project. We round off by looking at the field of usability and user experience (UX) research where rigorous research protocols and testing methods inform user-centred design, and considering what placemakers could learn from these practices.

2.2	THINKING LIKE A RESEARCHER

Impartiality, ethical practice, reliability and validity are the fundamental principles underpinning all aspects of social research. They apply in any research field where the principal subject of study is human activity – including gathering material to help design places that will be used by people. Attending to these principles will raise the methodological rigour of participation programmes in spatial design. This means gathering better information, and from that gaining more useful knowledge to work into a scheme, which means better design outcomes. I'd like to stress that research, information-gathering and engagement should be integral to the design process. The point is to have reliable, valid, useful knowledge to work with from the earliest possible stage, which is built up as the project evolves. Selecting the right methods to provide the right information at the right time should be ongoing work that's part and parcel of design development. So with that in mind, what do these principles mean?

Impartiality

The impartiality principle refers to a researcher's obligation to operate from as neutral and objective a position as possible, without favouring any group or viewpoint. Clearly, this may not always translate comfortably into the built environment sector; designers often consult on their own designs, clients want to muster local support for a proposal, and commercial pressures and political agendas can also muddy the waters. As this book is about working effectively in the real world, it focuses on objectively gathering information and working within these boundaries, rather than achieving methodological nirvana.

Impartiality is essential, particularly in communications. It means being clear about the programme's aims and outcomes, and open as to what can and cannot be changed in the proposal. All public communications should be worded in neutral, easily understood language, giving people the information they need to make up their own minds. The designer-researcher's role within this context is to understand local needs and wishes, to listen to opinions and feelings without trying to influence them, to view the data objectively, and to produce plans based on that evidence offering the best deal for the community.

Ethical practice

Ethical practice is all about the rights and responsibilities of researchers and participants (designers and communities in this context). The key elements of research ethics that apply in community participation are treating participants with respect and dignity, and maintaining high standards of integrity and professionalism; again, treating the community as the client. Ethical practice is at the heart of inclusive placemaking. Consider ethical issues at every stage of the research strategy, from setting the objectives to deciding who to involve and how to communicate findings. Think of ethics not as rules on what *not* to do but pointing to what *could* be done better to promote inclusion and maximise participation. How this translates into practice depends on the nature of the proposals and the local community, but should be an integral part of the thinking on every aspect of a participation programme in any type of project.

Ethical practice has particular relevance in designing with, rather than for, marginalised groups. There's more in Chapter 9 about working with people with disabilities and sensory or cognitive impairments, as well as social and cultural exclusion issues that a wide range of groups experience. There's also specific guidance on working with children and young people, where ethical practice is non-negotiable, particularly in issues around informed consent and safeguarding requirements.

Reliability

Moving away from community relationships now, reliability and validity are about data quality and analysis. The measure of validity is that if a study was run again by another team the results and findings would be pretty much the same. This requires that information is collected and analysed without bias as far as possible. 'Bias' usually refers to prejudice or favouritism in everyday parlance, but in a research context it denotes any kind of skew that potentially impacts on accuracy. And skew is inevitable. There are two main types, which are as relevant to a community participation programme as to an anthropological study or psychological experiment:

1. **Researcher bias** is when a researcher's preconceptions may lead them to misinterpret or misrepresent data. This also includes methodological bias, which refers to aspects of the research process itself that could affect the data collection or analysis.

2. **Participant bias** is the influence of factors on participants that consciously or unconsciously affects their responses, such that they may not be a true reflection of their values or behaviour.

Awareness of bias and a commitment to minimising it are integral to thinking like a researcher. In a spatial design context, participation programmes are commonly skewed by the questions asked (methodological bias), the people asked (participant bias) and a lack of impartiality (researcher bias). Each research method chapter (Chapters 3 to 8) includes a section on bias issues associated with that approach, with an extensive list of biases defined in the Appendix. Forewarned is forearmed.

So how can designers gather reliable information from relevant people with minimal bias?

Firstly, the research strategy should be appropriate to the type of development and local communities. This means relevant, accessible approaches which provide the greatest opportunity for participation; a mix of quantitative and qualitative methods maximises participation opportunities.

Secondly, reliable research requires good sampling, which can mean aiming for quality rather than quantity of input. Getting feedback from as many people as possible might seem like the obvious goal, but capturing a full spectrum of views and hearing from a wide range of groups is just as important – which a high volume of responses doesn't necessarily provide. It's good practice to proactively contact groups who are known to be less likely to engage and go to meet them in the early stages to hear about issues affecting them, discuss the proposals, and encourage them to contribute. Identify any barriers that could discourage or prevent people in so-called 'hard-to-reach' groups from participating. In all this pre-launch work, it pays dividends to start discussions with the community as early as possible.

Hard-to-reach groups	Many take issue with the term 'hard to reach'; it has connotations of blaming excluded groups for failing to engage rather than the systems that exclude them. I refer to 'marginalised groups' here instead, highlighting the ethical responsibility to include and serve these communities.
	Examples, but not an exhaustive list, of groups who may be marginalised with particular regard to public space and the urban environment include (in no particular order): people with mobility, cognitive or sensory impairments; people with chronic health problems or physical disabilities; young people; older people; LGBT people; ethnic or cultural minorities; refugees and asylum seekers; people with learning disabilities; people with mental health problems; homeless people; travellers; people in insecure employment or housing, and people with low literacy.

Validity

Validity is about translating the research objectives into effective, actionable questions, and finding valid ways to gain the information required to answer those questions – or operationalisation for short. It's also about correctly interpreting data and correctly applying it when there are conclusions to be drawn, findings to be reported and recommendations to be made.

In a community participation context, validity means asking the right questions and measuring the right things to get the relevant data, then looking objectively at what it's saying and drawing findings from this evidence that reflect the setting and community at that time and place as accurately as possible. With quantitative material from surveys, this might mean identifying correlations and patterns, for instance. Qualitative material may be more challenging, as it doesn't always offer up clear answers to the research questions. This makes impartiality all the more important in putting aside preconceived ideas or hoped-for results and aiming for good validity.

2.3	CREATING A RESEARCH STRATEGY

Equipped with these eternal verities of social research practice, we can now use them as the foundation of a project research strategy. A research strategy sets objectives and research questions at the outset, and gives clarity and purpose to the project's information-gathering work; see Figure 2.1. This is common practice in UX and product design research, and many built environment practices already do the same thing in their community engagement work too, in different ways and under various names. I'll continue with 'research strategy' and 'research objectives' here, however, as they carry a reminder of the methodological planning that underpins data gathering and the need for a structured approach to working with the information.

A research strategy document guides a project and mainly consists of answers to the questions: 'What do we need to know?', 'Who can provide the information we need?' and 'How shall we gather and analyse this information?', which should be addressed in that order. These are discussed in the next sections, and there's a sample document template bringing them together (see p. 22). The research strategy defines a project's scope and rationale. Talking about product design, for instance, Gyoko Muratovski makes a forceful case for getting the strategy right from the start: 'At the heart of every design project lays a problem. The ability to understand this problem is paramount to the success of the design outcome. If you do not understand exactly what this problem is, you will not be able to design a solution that can address this problem.' (Muratovski, 2016, p. 29).

Figure 2.1
Developing the research
strategy

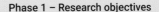

Phase 1 – Research objectives

What do we need to know? (And why?)
↓
Define up to three research objectives ('This research will ...')

↓

Phase 2 – Operationalisation

Translate the research objectives into 6–10 answerable questions
↓
What sort of data is needed to answer these questions?
↓
Who can provide it? (Sampling)
↓
What are the best techniques to capture and analyse that data?
↓
Check the data can be analysed within the time and resources available
↓
Finalise methodology

↓

Phase 3 – Strategy

Add in timescale, roles and responsibilities, outline of rationale/need, etc
↓
Draft a detailed strategy (see Figure 2.2)
↓
Keep under review – adapt and update as needed

First question: What do we need to know?

To establish the research objectives, just complete the sentence 'This research will ...' in broad terms. There should be no more than three objectives. In relation to a public space, as a very simplistic example, they might be something like:

1. Understand the site context and functions that the site currently serves.
2. Find out what people want/need/would like to see there.
3. Identify some possible options for the site.

The next stage is to draft six to ten questions for the research to answer, which operationalise the objectives into specific areas of study. Each research question should have a defined focus, not overlap with any others and, obvious though it may sound, be answerable from the information likely to be available. In the UX field, Tomer Sharon advises asking not only 'What do we want to know?' but also 'Why?' (Sharon, 2015). This means considering whether questions will actually yield the information required (in other words, do they have validity?) As the project progresses it's worth noting the work that's been done on each research question, to ensure there's a sufficient amount of material for each.

Finally, build an evaluation strategy into the programme from the start. Evaluation should measure the quantity and quality of engagement. Getting plenty of people involved is good, but less so if only the 'usual suspects' get to express their views. Monitoring participant feedback is essential, so gather responses to events, activities, websites, surveys and communications through quick evaluation questionnaires and by simply asking people informally how they are finding the process. The final element to the evaluation strategy is sharing and building on the knowledge gained, so that the team, participants and wider public and professional audiences can learn from the experience.

Second question: Who can provide the information we need?

With the research objectives, research questions and evaluation strategy defining what we want to know, it's now time to identify who can best provide the information we need. Sampling, in research terms, is selecting data sources from which to draw in a research project. These could be individuals, households, groups, locations or any other defined source. The nature of the project, the context, the client's requirements and logistical considerations will all influence sampling decisions, which may have to reflect what can realistically be achieved rather than gold-standard methodology. Nonetheless, aim for a wide range of sources. Getting the sampling right isn't just a matter of methodological quality: it can determine whether people view the programme as lip service or genuine. Some types of development will require contacting every household affected and inviting them to give their views; this can be the case for schemes in residential areas, for instance. As a general rule, if it's feasible to contact everyone affected, then do. Public realm projects are less clear-cut; for example, it won't always be known who will use a proposed space, in which case it's better to seek a cross-section of community opinion instead.

Participation specialists advise a little caution in working with community groups. Leaders or spokespeople don't always speak for everyone, or necessarily even the majority. And the people who can offer the most valuable insights aren't always the first to come forward. It's better to talk to a few people and assess the range of views, so start informal conversations before the formal programme launches wherever possible, to gain more understanding of the group and their issues, and ensure they're well informed about the project. As these groups are likely to be volunteer-run, with scant resources and other priorities, starting discussions early can make their participation easier and more likely, by identifying aspects of the proposals relevant to them, discussing any particular concerns, and agreeing how they'll give feedback.

Third question: How shall we gather and analyse this information?

The final stage is deciding how to gather data from the required sources that will yield the required information: in other words, methodology. Only consider methodology after defining the objectives, research questions and who to involve. Never start with a preferred approach; the research aims will point to the best ways. A reverse-engineering approach can help to decide appropriate methods; that is, start by identifying the outputs that are needed and then work back to see how best to deliver them. The essential thing is to choose approaches that produce information that will help answer the research questions and that will allow all relevant groups to contribute.

The subsequent chapters cover a selection of established methods – by no means an exhaustive list, as new approaches are developing all the time, especially as technology evolves – but sufficient for most situations. Researchers often favour a mix of methods: quantitative methods providing statistics on when, what, where and how many, and qualitative for insights on why and how. Using mixed methods has the added benefit of offering people a range of ways to participate. Remember only to source material that will be usable. After collecting hours of video recordings or observation notes, for instance, staff need to have the time and skills to review, transcribe, analyse and interpret it all.

Before putting these questions together to form the research strategy, I want to stress that a participation programme isn't merely a data-mining exercise. All this information-gathering should be taking place in the context of collaborative and mutually beneficial relationships with the community. It's important to give local

Figure 2.2
Research strategy template

Background

- Inception and rationale for the proposed development
- Client background

Context

- Site context; any other relevant proposals
- Local context, e.g. socio-economic factors
- Local community, e.g. demographics, key stakeholders, community groups and others with an interest, main concerns

Research objectives

- Up to three statements of the project's intended outcomes, starting 'This research will ...'

Research questions

- 6–10 answerable questions that operationalise the objectives into specific topics

Methodology

- Methods of gathering data to answer the research questions, with rationale

Participants

- Local individuals, organisations, groups and stakeholders who should be involved
- The level of participation on offer and the stages at which people will be able to contribute
- How participants will be contacted / how the programme will be publicised for maximum engagement
- Any ethical issues, e.g. risk assessment, confidentiality, informed consent, working with children or vulnerable groups

Evaluation

- Processes for monitoring participation and receiving participants' feedback on the programme
- Processes for evaluating the effectiveness of the programme and approaches
- Processes for sharing lessons learned and using knowledge that was gained

Schedule

- Timetable, key dates and deadlines for the project

Outputs

- Planning documents, report to client, feedback to participants, online/media content, etc.

Resources

- Human resources, time and costs involved
- Roles and responsibilities

groups space to talk to each other, to develop relationships and to build capacity. Look for opportunities that could attract funders, sponsors and organisations that could contribute in other ways to the programme and/or the community. If designers see themselves as enablers rather than providers, the emphasis shifts to helping local communities realise their ambitions, instead of designing *for* them. This is why gaining and demonstrating an understanding of local concerns and agendas is such an important starting point: participation then has relevance and benefits from the outset.

Putting the strategy together

Having finalised the research objectives, research questions, sampling approach and methodology, we now have the main elements of the research strategy. This suggested template at Figure 2.2 brings them together and should work with small or large-scale projects, adapted as required. (The Background and Context information can be gathered from existing project documentation and desk research.)

Creating a data library

A participation programme will generate a considerable amount of material as it progresses. There will be content produced by participants such as survey responses, consultation feedback, diaries, outputs from workshops and community events, and evaluation forms. There will be material produced by the team, such as mapping and counting datasets, photos, videos, transcripts and record sheets from public meetings and events. And there will be general content like correspondence, publicity materials, reports and notes from meetings. So much material in so many formats can be a lot to keep track of, so, if possible, set up a project data library to manage it all. Create a spreadsheet or some central record to catalogue the material, recording details like the date created, the type of material, a short content description, keywords and any other details to help identify or locate material: see Figure 2.3. How this is implemented depends on the practice set-up and the nature of the project; whatever adaptations are required, the bottom line is to log everything in a way that allows a search across the whole collection of material.

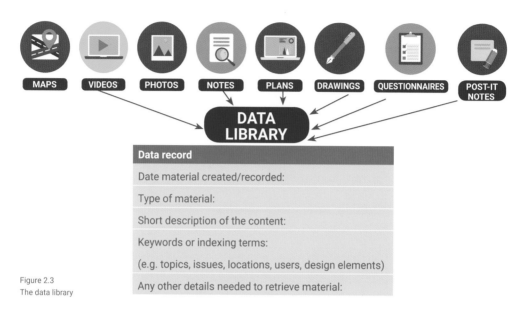

Figure 2.3
The data library

A second essential resource that's needed from the start is a contacts database. This will hold details of local stakeholders to be kept informed and invited to events, such as statutory consultees, key individuals, councillors, businesses, civic societies, residents' groups and community organisations. At the same time, set up a mailing list to send a news email and other updates to these contacts and anyone else who wants to receive it, and encourage people to sign up for email updates at public events and online.

2.4	**LESSONS FROM THE USER EXPERIENCE (UX) FIELD**

The UX field is way ahead of the built environment sector in terms of user-centred design. Research processes are relatively simple but they give designers good evidence of users' needs and wants, so that they can design accordingly. I mentioned in the previous chapter how product design and UX research put new products through rigorously evaluated research cycles of prototyping, testing, redesign and re-testing. The built environment's a different world, of course, but spatial designers can learn much from these user-focused fields. Surely if developers of mobile apps or websites attend so closely to users' responses to these relatively ephemeral creations, shouldn't designers of spaces intended to last for years to come listen more carefully to their users?

Usability and user experience research

Research processes in product design and UX point the way to improvements in spatial design practice in two areas in particular: starting with the user in mind, and Involving users early on in the planning and design process. The point of UX research is to enable informed design decisions, which means greater user satisfaction, more customers and a healthy bottom line. UX is considered to pay serious dividends in some design fields. At IBM, for example, every $1 invested in user research reportedly generates $10–100 in profit, because usable products are the most efficient and the most commercially successful (Muratovski, 2016). User-centred design involves research at each stage of the design process and beyond, measuring usability and gathering feedback post-launch – just as important in the research cycle as pre-launch testing.

Research in consumer products starts by gathering data on users' priorities, needs and wants: asking how and when a product will be used, its must-have functions and other desirable features. The UX pioneer Jakob Nielsen recommends a seven-step process for usability testing (Nielsen, 2012), summarised below, which although aimed at designers in technology and digital sectors, has clear relevance to spatial design. He argues that user testing shouldn't wait until detailed designs are ready, because by this point most critical usability problems are likely to require major redesign to rectify. So involving users early on is essential. Note that in Nielsen's seven steps, design development only starts halfway through the process.

Nielsen's seven steps of usability testing, from inception to completion:

1. Before starting a new design, **identify good features in the previous design** that are worth keeping, as well as features that are problematic for users.

2. **Look at relevant designs by others** to see what works and what doesn't.

3. **Conduct field research** to understand how users behave in their natural habitat.

4. **Create very basic prototypes** of new design ideas and begin usability testing.

5. **Identify which design ideas test best**, and develop more detailed iterations, testing at each stage.

6. **Assess the designs** against established usability guidelines.

7. **Decide and implement the final design**. Test again once it's live; unforeseen usability problems still often occur after completion.

Prototypes can be tested on-screen and/or as a basic physical model. Researchers draw on a combination of methods, usually including observation, diary studies, questionnaires, focus groups, individual interviews and task-based exercises to study users' responses, the features they liked, those they didn't need or understand, ease of use, and so on. (It is no coincidence that many of those research methods appear in this book's chapter listing). The design is then refined and re-tested, informed by test results at each stage, until it reaches optimal functionality and user satisfaction. Once the product does everything that users need and want, the final 'look and feel' can be decided. Yes, aesthetic considerations come last.

Another approach worth considering is heuristic evaluation, where designers assess an initial concept design against mutually agreed usability criteria before testing. This allows many usability problems to be resolved at the outset, and then each iteration evolves the design in response to user test feedback. Could designers in the built environment adopt similar processes to allow greater certainty as to whether their designs will be well received? Could it become standard placemaking procedure to start by creating prototype models that allow potential users to explore features and functionality, collecting detailed feedback, adjusting the model to incorporate their responses, testing again, getting more feedback, finally achieving maximum usability and functionality – and *then* working on the design details?

2.5	KEY POINTS SUMMARY

> Applying the key social research principles of impartiality, ethical practice, reliability and validity improves community participation programmes. Greater methodological rigour in these processes benefits everyone.

These principles can translate readily into good practice in working with local communities on spatial design, especially in terms of gathering and analysing data, and communications.

There are three questions to ask at the start of a project, in this order.

1. 'What do we need to know?' defines the objectives for the project, which can then be operationalised into research questions.

2. 'Who can provide the information we need?' means considering the whole range of people who could be affected by a development, being clear about whose voices need to be heard – whether the 'silent majority' or marginalised groups – and doing everything possible to bring them into the process.

3. Then, and only then, consider 'How should we gather and analyse that information?' A mix of qualitative and quantitative methods produces a more rounded picture and greater understanding, but requires more time and analytical work.

Having decided on appropriate research methods, draft a research strategy that summarises aims, methods and required outputs.

There are two essential information management resources to create at the start: a central data library to hold all the project material, and a contacts database.

Usability testing methods could benefit spatial design, particularly by adopting processes of prototyping, testing and refining usability and user satisfaction before starting detailed design.

Meaningful participation programmes start with an understanding of where people are coming from, building trust and rapport, and communicating clearly and honestly.

Desire Lines: A Guide to Community Participation in Designing Places

3   # Observation

'It is difficult to design a space that will not attract people – what is remarkable is how often this has been accomplished.'

– William H. Whyte

3.1	**INTRODUCTION**

It's no coincidence that the most influential social studies of modern urban public space have started with street-level observation. Jane Jacobs' analysis of the American city's daily 'sidewalk ballet' (1961), William H. Whyte's documentation of the social life of New York public spaces (1980), and Jan Gehl's ongoing inquiry into human interactions with the urban built environment have all changed the course of mainstream thinking about how cities should work. And as Gehl and Svarre (2013) argue, this has been achieved only by being out on the street, systematically observing what people do in the real world.

Observation as a research technique derives from anthropology, the study of humans as social animals in their natural settings. It gives designers rich opportunities to understand real life behaviour and activity in all its complexity, and to examine people's relationships with places and environments; for instance, product design and UX use observation extensively to see how people use products and to test prototypes. However, observation alone doesn't provide an adequate basis for decision-making. It complements other research methods but offers no voice or influence to end-users. This chapter looks at applications for observation techniques, some approaches to gathering qualitative and quantitative data from observation, and working with the material gathered.

OBSERVATION

Methodology type:
qualitative | quantitative

Level of participation:
none

Time/resource needed for data collection:
high

Time/resource needed for data analysis:
high

Useful for:
understanding site context

understanding behaviour/interactions/use of space

site planning/generating ideas

3.2   **OBSERVATION-BASED APPROACHES**

Participant and non-participant observation

There are two distinct approaches to observation: participant and non-participant (or naturalistic). This chapter focuses on non-participant observation, as it's more appropriate for the type of research questions that designers are likely to ask. It entails observing people's behaviour in real-world settings, fly-on-the-wall style, and was integral to the landmark studies mentioned above. As 'non-participant observation' implies, researchers unobtrusively observe people in their everyday lives, doing whatever they normally do, uninfluenced by the researcher's presence. This can take either a structured approach to gather mainly quantitative data or an unstructured approach to gather qualitative data (see Figure 3.1).

Structured observation

Structured observations tend to focus on human activity that can be systematically mapped, counted and measured. This might then be used to assess pedestrian volumes or common routes, or gain insight into specific topics like the types of activities in a space, how long people stay there, or demographic trends, perhaps. Information from structured observation can also inform decisions on aspects of a design or site layout. Do features within a space create physical barriers or encourage interaction? Do the ways that different groups use the same space conflict?

Figure 3.1
Types of
observation

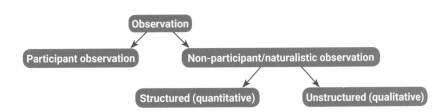

Some observations can be undertaken perfectly effectively using the low-cost no-frills techniques favoured by Gehl: human observers, in-situ, with pen and paper. There's the added benefit of having people on the ground who are able to help interpret anything unclear. Complex sites or large-scale projects are likely to require more sophisticated survey technology. GPS, CCTV and the like allow the collection of much greater volumes of data over longer time periods, with counting and mapping automated or done remotely. Both hi-tech and low-tech strategies should produce the same result, however, namely reliable data that provides a foundation for evidence-based decision-making.

Unstructured observation

Unstructured observation offers real benefits in the exploratory phase at the start of a project. Effective observers can provide valuable insight into local social-spatial dynamics to help the team understand the realities of the site context and to consider options for the site in this light. At the same time, it's also an excellent way to begin developing ideas about approaches to engaging with the local population, keeping the location, the community and the new development at the forefront. It gives observers the freedom to note anything that might pertain to the research questions, and allows them to form their own impressions of a site's significant aspects rather than starting with a list of things on which to focus. Of course, designers don't need to be told to look round a site beforehand and scope it out for themselves, so isn't that an unstructured observation? The difference is methodological rigour. Observation is purposeful and focused, guided by defined research objectives, yielding copious notes and other records, which are methodically analysed in depth. So it's much more than just having a look round!

EXAMPLE   A project took place to assess the need for traffic management measures in a small town near Sheffield. This began with a consultation team from Local Level undertaking an unstructured observation to provide an initial understanding of the main traffic issues. Observing the streets at different times of day and throughout the week enabled them to identify the locations of the main traffic problems and to decide the next steps. The findings from the observation data informed the decision to survey local residents and businesses in the affected locations, and to use the insight from that survey data to formulate some possible solutions to put out for wider consultation.

| 3.3 | **PREPARATION** |

Figure 3.2
Suggested observation process

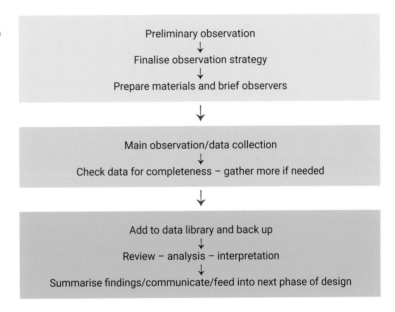

Preliminary observation
↓
Finalise observation strategy
↓
Prepare materials and brief observers

↓

Main observation/data collection
↓
Check data for completeness – gather more if needed

↓

Add to data library and back up
↓
Review – analysis – interpretation
↓
Summarise findings/communicate/feed into next phase of design

Preliminary observation

If possible, members of the design/observation team should undertake a preliminary observation visit to inform the observation proper. This will clarify its aims and parameters, defining the questions it will be answering, and deciding how to capture the information those questions require. This should include quantitative work, such as:

- mapping and photographing the site
- identifying the main routes and active areas
- selecting observation locations
- setting the boundaries of the observation site.

There is also qualitative work to do towards understanding the socio-spatial context, for example noting visual and sensory impressions, sketching, watching interactions and behaviour, and generally starting to think like a researcher. Having clarified the observation's aims and scope, the team should then be able to finalise the strategy and decide roles, timing and duration of observation periods, and identify resources required. Figure 3.2 shows a suggested process for the whole exercise.

Remember that the logistics of data gathering influence the information yielded. Factors like time constraints, observers' locations and decisions on what to count or map often have implications, so consider what these could be. Observers will need an outline map of the study area showing the main paths and features within the space, and a reference sheet, tested out first whenever possible, setting out how everything should be recorded. Run a briefing session beforehand to ensure that observers will work consistently. It's sensible at this point to discuss situations that could potentially arise for them, such as responding to questions about their activities, dealing with people who object to being watched or recorded, and personal safety concerns. Unlikely eventualities, but it's better for observers to be prepared.

Bias issues

At the data-gathering stage, an unstructured observation can be influenced by observers' preconceptions or misinterpretation. A structured observation can also yield flawed information by not including significant aspects of a site, ignoring types of users or overlooking types of use. Later, at the analysis stage, observers can be prone to jumping-to-conclusions types of errors, only seeing what they expected, or misattributing causes or meanings to what they've observed. These kinds of errors tend to occur when unquestioned assumptions or selective attention impacts on the data gathering or analysis, and are inevitable to some degree. Ascribing meaning or causality where meaning and causality cannot be known are constant temptations in an uncertain world, but have no place in methodologically robust research.

So how can these biases be tackled? A good level of self-awareness, integrity and attention to detail always make a successful observation possible. It might help to employ Popper's method of falsification or refutability (Popper, 1959), whereby researchers play their own devil's advocate and look for explanations to disprove their theories rather than evidence to support them. Another solution is to ask others to review the material and see if they arrive at similar conclusions. I would also endorse Gehl and Svarre's advice on addressing an historical imbalance; disabled people, elderly people, women and children have been routinely overlooked throughout decades of urban planning and placemaking, so pay extra attention to these groups to redress the deficit.

BIAS ISSUES IN OBSERVATION

One of the most important tasks during the preparation phase is to consider where bias could occur. Observers are human and fallible, public space is a complex place and appearances can be deceptive, so these inherent pitfalls need to be considered. Types of bias that are most likely to occur in observation-based research are:

PLANNING
Exclusion bias | Selection bias
Who does the observation include and not include?

DATA COLLECTION
Measurement bias | Observer bias
Will the counting or measurement methods yield valid and reliable data?

ANALYSIS
Clustering illusion | Confirmation bias | Culture bias | Focusing effect |
Illusory correlation | Observer-expectancy effect | Stereotyping
Are observers seeing only what they expected to see or is unexpected data also coming to light? Have observers recognised their own preconceptions and ways of seeing? Can apparent relationships between data be substantiated? Are patterns significant or random?

See the Appendix for explanations of these types of bias.

3.4	GATHERING OBSERVATION MATERIAL

Counting

Counting generates quantitative data on human activity in a space, useful for finding out things such as the times of main usage, who uses the space, whether there's a broad or narrow range of users, the features that people do and don't use, and the types of events and activity that occur there. These kinds of statistics can be a worthwhile addition to an evidence base informing decisions about a project, and provide baseline data to assess a scheme's impact post-completion. Although counting can reveal patterns of activity, it doesn't offer explanations. Nor can observers always identify with certainty what people are doing just by watching them. Interpretations are therefore usually provisional.

Jan Gehl (2011) characterises two types of activity in public space worth recording in structured or unstructured observation:

1. **Necessary**. Purposeful and goal-orientated activities such as essential shopping, and work-related journeys or tasks.

2. **Optional**. More leisurely or informal activities such as strolling, eating, playing, sitting, reading or chatting.

Gehl recommends noting the locations where optional activity occurs, especially the places where people choose to sit or stay – whether on the edges of a space or in the middle, in secluded areas or out in the open, for example – as signifying features that people value, such as sun, shade, sight lines and proximity to other activity. (Whyte, 1980, suggests the number of women sitting alone in a public space can indicate the sense of safety it offers, which may or may not be worth keeping in mind.) The ratio of necessary-to-optional activities show whether its character is primarily functional, enabling mainly necessary activity or whether its features encourage optional activities.

Activity can be measured by two main counting methods. The nature of the space, the topics of interest and the research questions will largely decide which is appropriate (it may be both).

1. **Time-based counts** note how many times particular activities or events occur in a given timeframe

2. **Interval-based counts** note everything that's happening at given times during the day, for example, every 30 minutes.

A hand-held click-counter can be useful in busy spaces with large numbers of people; otherwise a pad and pen, or a pre-printed table or checklist to mark up should suffice. It's best to undertake counts at different times of day and in different seasonal conditions, which means it can take several weeks or longer to gather sufficient data. Whatever the approach, it's essential that all observers work consistently, counting and recording in the same ways.

Mapping

Mapping generates quantitative data on movement paths through a space, such as pedestrian flows and routes. It provides information on stationary behaviour too, showing areas where people linger and those they avoid. It can highlight problems in accessing the space, such as a lack of road crossings or clear paths, or hindrances within the space itself, such as steps or inconveniently placed fixtures. Again, undertake mapping exercises at different times of day and in different conditions, and if possible over several weeks. As with counting, mapping movement in and around a space can provide good baseline evidence to inform decision-making, and assess the completed scheme.

Data can be collected by one or both of these approaches:

1. **Time-based mapping,** when observers trace the routes taken through or around a space, recording individuals' approximate paths on a map. Although inexact, it can provide a clear enough picture of primary and secondary routes, and paths less travelled. In spaces with large numbers of people, some systematic random sampling may be necessary: tracking every Nth person who enters, perhaps.

2. **Interval-based mapping,** when observers mark up a map at specific time intervals to show the locations of different groups of users and types of activities at that moment, using an agreed notation. These produce an aggregated picture over the whole time period when merged, so this method provides information on users, activities and both datasets combined.

Gehl and Svarre also suggest measuring walking speed in pedestrianised settings as an indicator of the quality of a space, on the basis that a slower pace indicates a more enjoyable environment. Calculate this by finding an observable stretch of walkable space and measuring out a section of approximately 100 metres, then measuring with a stopwatch the time it takes randomly selected pedestrians to walk from end to end. They also recommend test walks, where observers walk key routes themselves, noting positive and negative features along the way. This can highlight some considerable differences in walkability between how a route looks on a plan and the reality on the ground. For example, a test walk for a study they undertook in Sydney produced the gloomy finding that 52% of the total walking time on one route was spent waiting at pedestrian crossings.

Photography and video

Video and still photographs can record structured or unstructured observations to provide an accessible visual documentation of a space and the nature of activity within it. This can contextualise other quantitative information, or provide a data source itself. For example, a series of captures of a particular activity can reveal new information about that activity when images are examined together afterwards. Images might be recorded to a brief, to address specific research questions or to capture particular types of events, or could adopt a less structured approach to depict a range of aspects or qualities of a space. The AEIOU mnemonic (Martin and Hanington, 2012) is a useful reminder for observers to document:

> **A**ctivities
> **E**nvironments
> **I**nteractions
> **O**bjects
> **U**sers

Shoot more images or footage than is strictly needed, as aspects can be noticed in review that were missed on site, so it's sometimes helpful to have extra material to examine. Aesthetic value is of no importance here; images just need to be clear, well lit and properly exposed. In a small space, a smartphone may be suitable for recording video or stills if the image quality is adequate, and will attract less attention (and therefore potentially influence people's behaviour) than a video or camera.

Photography or video recording for observation exercises requires discretion and sensitivity; even in a public space, there are ethical issues to consider and limits to what it's acceptable to shoot. It's legal to photograph people or anything else from a public space without consent, but this can still be an invasion of personal privacy. If in doubt, let people know that you're documenting the general environment, not them personally. Whyte recommends not recording people in ignominious situations or in the midst of personal difficulties, or engaged in any kind of illicit activity, even if these do take place in public.

Simulation and experiential monitoring

It is now possible to record individuals' cognitive and emotional responses as well as their patterns of movement. Thanks to rapidly evolving technology utilising various types of sensor linked to a phone app or portable device that can monitor brainwave patterns, heartbeat, eye movements and breathing, people's responses to different real-world environments can be measured, showing the levels of interest, pleasure or stress that their surroundings evoke. Similarly, experimental urban design research creates immersive virtual environments in laboratory settings to record people's physiological reactions to simulated urban spaces and experiences. An unprecedented depth of insight into wayfinding behaviour, cognition and the effects on mood that different street typologies and environments create is now available. Yet the director of one such research centre – Colin Ellard at the Urban Realities Laboratory based at the University of Waterloo in Canada – maintains that 'Although there is no doubting the power of a virtual reality simulation to unearth relationships between the organisation of the built environment and the operation of our minds ... there is no substitute for experimentation at street level' (Ellard, 2014). The knowledge generated from this field of research provides designers with exciting opportunities to create people-centred environments offering maximum enjoyment and interest, and minimum stress and anxiety, taking much of the guesswork out of whether the public will embrace or avoid a new space. Nonetheless, observation of real world street life, with its traffic, noise, smells, crowds, random interactions and unexpected occurrences remains indispensable.

3.5	WORKING WITH OBSERVATION MATERIAL

An observation exercise will generate a variety of types of material: maps, notes, drawings, diagrams and photos, at least. Ensure sufficient time is allowed for working through it all, as it can be complex and time-consuming to analyse in detail. So where to start? The first task is to add everything to the project data library. Catalogue the material, recording the type of content and the aspects of the project to which it relates, categorised by location, theme or user group, and specific tags or keywords to note particular events, for instance. This will form a useful resource to bring to further analysis, and in reports and publicity materials. It's best to create working copies of image and video files, and other documents, rather than to edit or annotate the originals. Check that all material is usable and complete; if not, collect what's needed to fill in any gaps before starting on the analysis.

Quantitative material, such as counts and maps, should be relatively straightforward to analyse and interpret if it was gathered with a clear purpose in mind, and the research questions should be able to provide a structure for analysis and reporting. Qualitative material from written notes, drawings, photos or video, is inherently more complex but still requires a structured analytical approach; refer to the 'Quick guide to analysing qualitative data' on p. 60 for a suggested process. Again, look to the research questions for analytical direction. It's important in the analysis stage to allow new ideas or questions that weren't covered by the initial research objectives to emerge, and to include rather than ignore things that weren't anticipated. Any observation project will encounter unexpected phenomena at some point, so it may be necessary to adapt the research strategy to accommodate the data, rather than vice versa.

Once all the material has been considered, which will require a few passes and consideration from different angles, some tentative interpretations may be starting to form. I stress 'tentative' interpretations. Observation studies at the start of a project don't normally need to provide answers, just useful information that can complement further research and inform the project as it develops. Additionally, while video, photography, mapping and counting give valuable baseline information, they don't necessarily provide explanations, as I've mentioned. No image can be taken at face value, and the camera can and does lie. So keep an open mind about photos and video.

Any conclusions drawn from observation work at this stage should derive directly and only from the material gathered; see the 'Quick guide to reporting research' (p. 136) for more guidance. Be transparent in reporting the results, and include anomalous or contradictory findings. The aim is to develop evidence to inform the design, so all data is potentially useful at this stage.

Observation data in design development

Space Syntax provided pedestrian movement and space usage data for Gustafson Porter + Bowman's award-winning redevelopment of Nottingham city centre's under-used Old Market Square. Mapping the observation data on people's routes through and around the square revealed a striking finding: more than three-quarters of pedestrians chose to walk around the outside of the square rather than taking the quicker route across it (see Figure 3.3). As Space Syntax explain, 'By studying the spatial layout of the square and observing patterns of movement and space use, we were able to show how the design of the space influenced human behaviour. We used this analysis to explain why the square was currently under-performing, especially in its central area, which 78% of pedestrians avoided.' The observation data was key to understanding how the space was used, and the extent to which the square's layout affected people's navigation of the area. With this insight, proposals were developed that improved pedestrian routes, increased activity, and provided a more inviting and inclusive space.

Figure 3.3
Pedestrian routes before development, Nottingham Old Market Square

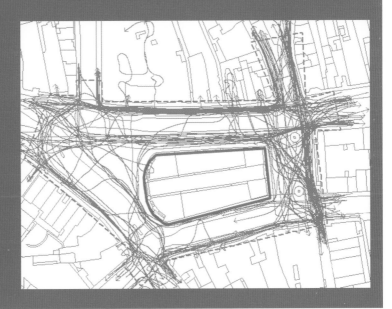

3.6	KEY POINTS SUMMARY

> Naturalistic or fly-on-the-wall style non-participant observation is the most suited to understanding how people use public space, and can yield valuable quantitative and qualitative data.

Structured observation is good for gathering data on specific topics or aspects of a space; unstructured observation gives the observer greater freedom to record what they choose.

Undertake a preliminary observation to understand the space and its issues, and inform the observation proper.

Opportunities for bias are plentiful. Be aware of observers' preconceptions, jumping to conclusions and the potential consequences of data collection logistics on the data and its interpretation.

Counting and mapping provide quantitative information on matters such as pedestrian numbers, primary routes, most and least used space, and types of activity.

Photography and video provide an essential visual record but video, in particular, requires time and care in analysis.

Several observers are better than one, and a combination of observation methods is also preferable.

Allow new ideas or questions that weren't in the initial research objectives to emerge, and be open to adapting the research strategy in light of unexpected findings.

Ensure sufficient time is allowed for working through observation data; it's a rich source of insight but complex and time-consuming to analyse in depth.

Desire Lines: A Guide to Community Participation in Designing Places

4　Diary studies

'We can't improve what we don't measure.'

−Anon

4.1	INTRODUCTION

In diary studies, people document specific aspects of their daily lives over a given time period, in their own words or images. This might be structured, using pre-set questions to research particular issues, or participants may be free to choose what to record. Diary studies can be useful at the start of a project to understand people's experiences, perceptions and behaviour patterns as they relate to a site or area. Unfiltered information-rich first-hand accounts can provide unique insights that other methods don't, and usefully complement quantitative methods, such as surveys. They can also be an effective way to engage with people who are less willing or able to participate in more public events. This chapter looks at the range of diary options, including text-based, image-based, online and offline, and the kinds of projects and participants they suit.

DIARY STUDIES

Methodology type:
qualitative | quantitative

Level of participation:
none

Time/resource needed for data collection:
low

Time/resource needed for data analysis:
medium

Useful for:
understanding site context
understanding attitudes/perceptions/values/feelings
understanding behaviour/interactions/use of space

4.2	**DIARY-BASED APPROACHES**

The diary study has long been an essential item in the social researcher's toolkit, and now occupies a similar role in UX research. It's not difficult to see why. Self-completed diaries show researchers how, when and why people use a product in real life, along with their feelings about it, the functions it fulfils for them, and their preferences for features and usability. Substituting 'place' for 'product', it's clearly a design research method with considerable potential in the built environment.

Diary-based methods can provide insight into issues like people's preferred spaces and routes, types of journeys, use of amenities and attitudes to local features. Participants can record their activities and experiences in text or images, or a mix, depending on the research objectives. Diary methods can also enable greater understanding of specific groups' experiences and daily lives; an example would be people with mobility or sensory impairments being asked to document the local environmental obstacles they encounter over a given period.

A **structured diary study**'s participants report on pre-set topics, yielding mainly quantitative material. This might be event-based, where they record a diary entry when they do a specific thing. For example, a scheme to upgrade a local play facility could use an event-based diary study to find out parents' views of the current facilities, asking them to make a record whenever they visit with their children. Alternatively, a time-based study might ask participants to complete the same questions each day for a short period, which can offer insight into the frequency of events or activities. A project looking at neighbourhood cohesion might ask a sample of residents to keep a diary of interactions with neighbours for a couple of weeks, for instance.

In an **unstructured diary study**, participants themselves decide what to record. This provides mainly qualitative material and works best with small samples, due to the time required for the analysis process. The earlier example of participants with disabilities documenting issues in their everyday journeys would be suitable for an unstructured approach, and would give individuals the freedom to decide what they want to discuss according to their personal experiences. There are suggestions as to how this example and the other two above could work in practice at the end of section 4.4 on p. 54.

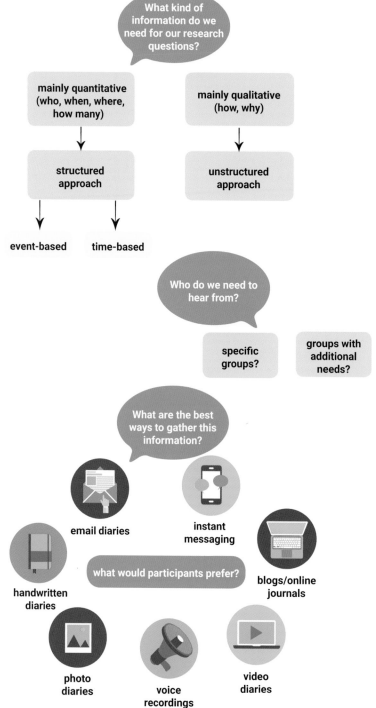

Figure 4.1
What type of diary
study to use?

Some participants will be more comfortable with image-based diary projects, where they submit photos or videos. This presents fewer language, literacy or learning ability barriers, and can engage a wide range of people. Others will prefer to express themselves in writing. If it's possible to offer a choice, ask participants at the outset which method they'd prefer, as this will improve participation and response rates. Figure 4.1 should help identify what types of diary studies might be appropriate for a project. Whatever the format, make sure diary tasks will maintain participants' interest over the study period, without being onerous or time-consuming for them, to minimise drop-out. Diaries can provide designers with a wealth of valuable information, but at the non-participation end of the spectrum this method doesn't give participants a direct influence on decision-making, while asking them to devote quite a bit of time to the task. Participants in commercial research of this kind are often given a small cash payment or vouchers on completion to thank them for their time and effort, so look at appropriate ways to reward participants.

Written diaries

Written diaries are a time-honoured research method, in which participants record a handwritten account of their activities over a specified period. This method has a directness and natural quality that participants often prefer, especially those less confident with technology. A written diary's advantages are portability and not requiring online access, so participants can update at almost any time and while memories are still easily recalled. It's a simple low-cost method and requires minimal briefing; for a structured approach with standard questions, participants often appreciate pre-printed diary sheets or prepared notebooks to fill in.

As for drawbacks, the material can be reviewed only once diaries have been submitted. Transcription can be time-consuming, and legibility and ambiguity can present issues. Furthermore, diarists may omit things they take for granted but that researchers would want to know about, so it's sensible to allocate some time post-submission for follow-up contacts in case more detail or clarification is needed. Unstructured qualitative diary studies are more appropriate to small-scale research projects, due to the time involved in transcription and analysis. Structured diaries, on the other hand, can collect more quantitative data on a greater scale, but may not yield the same level of insight.

Email diaries

Email diaries can be used either to record answers to structured questions on specific topics, or as a traditional journal where participants choose what to include. This makes for a versatile method, suitable for small-scale qualitative or large-scale quantitative information gathering. Email diaries offer the same advantages as written diaries in their potential for insight and ease of completion for most people, with some added benefits for researchers.

This is an easy format for most people to work with. If participants send in responses daily, it's possible to start reviewing material immediately, and to contact people with any queries while they still have a reasonable recall of events. Reminders can be sent to chase up late submissions, and there's scope to build rapport with participants, which should help to improve response rates and reduce drop-out rates. No transcription is required, and the material is easily prepared for review and analysis. Technology, language, or literacy factors may present difficulties for some, however, and participants may forget details if they don't make entries soon after the event. As with written diaries, meanings may be unclear and participants may omit details of interest.

Online platforms

New online possibilities emerge all the time. Social media, instant messaging services and other apps can all host diary studies. Participants can post images and video as well as text, and familiarity will be an advantage for many. These platforms also enable interaction with participants during the study period, useful if clarification or more detail is necessary. It might be useful for participants to communicate with each other as well.

Diary studies can utilise numerous other digital options, from simple text messaging to online journal platforms, offering the same advantages and drawbacks as email diaries. They can be very accessible methods for many people and straightforward for participants to work with after some initial guidance. Online journals can provide considerable flexibility; they're suitable for collecting material at any scale, allowing either standardised questions or an unstructured format, and the option to include photos or videos. Sending a friendly daily reminder and regular thanks and encouragement should benefit response rates. It may be possible to start reviewing entries straight away and, as with email, no transcription is required and the content needs little preparation before it's ready to work with. Participants may not always be able to record experiences or observations immediately, so flawed recall may be a problem. And although accessible to the majority, there are those for whom the technology, or language or literacy factors, will present obstacles to participation.

Online diaries require less preparation than other methods in terms of briefing participants, although it's important they're clear about the purpose and what's needed. The main thing is to ensure the technology for receiving and managing responses functions correctly and provides a dataset that can be fully analysed, so piloting and testing are essential before the study goes live.

Photo and video diaries

Although lacking the descriptive nuance of written diaries, photos and videos can be revealing sources of information on many aspects of the local environment. They are versatile methods, which can work on an individual or group basis, on a single day or over a period of time, with set themes and questions or freestyle. And more than other methods, photos allow a follow-up group discussion by participants (covered in section 4.5, p. 57). Videos additionally give participants the opportunity to add their own commentary, which can provide a valuable new layer of information. For participants who are comfortable recording and narrating, video can facilitate a natural flow of ideas in a powerful channel for 'thinking out loud'. Voice recording can also work well in this way.

Photo diaries can give insight into the context and everyday experiences of local residents or regular users of a space. With fewer language or literacy barriers, these methods can allow wider participation than text-based diaries, and give children and young people in particular a chance to contribute. In the case of videos, some participants might be deterred by the technology or by personal reticence, and of course video footage takes much longer than other methods to process and analyse. Participants need guidance on what and what not to shoot, covering the research aims and ethical and safety issues. The temptation to perform may also be hard for some to resist.

GIS/GPS

Urban planning projects around the world are increasingly using GPS-based apps to crowdsource data on issues relating to travel, public space and land use options. Further possibilities for local people to feed their experiences or ideas directly into central databases via location-based technology to inform decision-making seem ripe for exploration. While some participants or groups may contribute enthusiastically, others may engage very little, so it may not be known whether the aggregated views expressed are representative. But these methods are developing rapidly and are well worth considering for larger-scale developments.

EXAMPLE	Schoolchildren in Oslo were consulted by the city council to find out what deterred them from walking or cycling to school. A game-style app was developed called 'Trafikkagenten' – 'traffic agents' – in which children took on the role of secret agents with a mission to identify hazards on their route to school, such as roads they found difficult to cross or places that felt unsafe. They recorded these locations by GPS in real time, with their personal data kept anonymous for ethical reasons. The programme design used gamification to promote immediate engagement, and undertook to respond directly and immediately where possible to children's expressed needs, instead of delivering top-down measures to which they had no input. (Larsson, 2016)

4.3	**PREPARATION**

Piloting

Piloting a diary study is essential. A small group of colleagues and/or friends will do; the point is to ensure that:

- the briefing and instructions are clear
- the study will yield the kind of material required
- the data can be stored effectively, and be readily prepared and analysed.

Ask the pilot participants for feedback afterwards on the overall experience and make any necessary adjustments, testing again if necessary. Perform some trial analysis from the pilot, then finalise an analysis guide in line with the research questions.

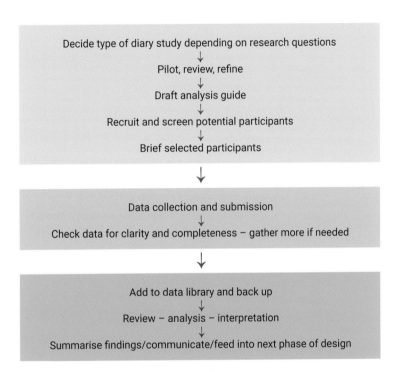

Decide type of diary study depending on research questions
↓
Pilot, review, refine
↓
Draft analysis guide
↓
Recruit and screen potential participants
↓
Brief selected participants

↓

Data collection and submission
↓
Check data for clarity and completeness – gather more if needed

↓

Add to data library and back up
↓
Review – analysis – interpretation
↓
Summarise findings/communicate/feed into next phase of design

Recruiting participants

Participant recruitment for written, email and photo/video diaries may need handling with care to ensure a high completion rate and good quality submissions. The research questions may require information from particular groups to find out about their experiences, or from a broad range of participants on more general themes. In any case, be selective about participants. As a general rule, less structured diary formats require greater selectivity in recruitment.

Make sure prospective participants understand the overall purpose of the exercise, their role within it and exactly what's involved, particularly for more detailed or qualitative approaches. The data collection period needs to suit participants while producing a usable amount of material; too long a study period can reduce take-up and increase drop-out rates. Ask for basic demographic details from the selected participants (for example, gender, age band and any other information relevant to the project, such as cultural background and any mobility or sensory impairments). Check they'll be able to submit in the required format and will be available for the time required; it's usual for 10–20% of recruits to drop out for various reasons, so plan accordingly.

Communication

Good communication is key to maintaining participants' motivation to complete diary tasks. If possible, speak to everyone individually before they start, explaining the process, checking they understand what's required from them and resolving any queries. If the exercise involves any privacy, safety or ethical issues, discuss them beforehand. You might want to advise against photographing or videoing friends or family members for confidentiality reasons, and warn against intruding on anyone's privacy or putting themselves in unsafe situations, for instance. Also, remind them the aim is to capture naturally occurring events, so nothing should be staged or exaggerated. However, avoid being too prescriptive; the idea is to see the world through their eyes and understand their perceptions and experiences, after all. Schedule phone or email contacts with participants at the beginning, in the middle and just before the end of the process, at least, to check on progress and offer thanks and encouragement. It will help keep everyone engaged and reminds participants that you value their work.

BIAS ISSUES IN DIARY STUDIES	Types of bias that can occur in diary studies are:
	PLANNING
	Exclusion bias | Selection bias
	Diary studies normally involve some prior screening, so consider how participant selection (and non-inclusion) could influence the data.
	DATA COLLECTION
	Attrition bias | Procedural bias
	Are there any practical or logistical issues that could affect participants' ability to complete the diary task satisfactorily? Some drop-out rate should be expected, but does the attrition rate still leave a complete and usable set of data?

ANALYSIS

Confirmation bias | Culture bias | Observer-expectancy effect |
Stereotyping

Are those undertaking the analysis making unexpected findings or only seeing what they thought they would see? It may be worth keeping the diary content anonymous and removing any demographic identifiers to avoid stereotyping or culturally conditioned interpretations.

PARTICIPANTS

Recall bias | Social desirability effect | Vividness effect

By the time diary entries are recorded, participants may have forgotten some aspects – or only recall the most vivid details – which can create bias. They may also record entries that reflect well on them, omitting views or behaviour that may not be judged favourably, so may not always represent full and truthful accounts.

See the Appendix for explanations of these types of bias.

4.4	GATHERING DIARY MATERIAL

Text-based diaries

Whether handwritten or electronic, structured diary entries normally include:

- **Basic quantitative information**: details of the when, where, who, how many, etc, as needed.
- **Observations relating to the research questions** include questions that operationalise the research objectives – for example, what activities were occurring, which aspects of the space were used.
- **Free text option or open-ended questions** include a space for any other observations not covered by the structured questions or participants' personal views if these can be used.

With an unstructured format, it helps to include some prompts for participants to remind them of the project's areas of interest. In-situ recording normally produces the most insightful material; participants often observe more actively, attend to detail more closely, and reflect more deeply when they record diary entries in real time. And if this isn't possible? If details may be vague or forgotten by the time they update their diaries, participants can take some photos as an aide-memoire, scribble some notes or make a voice recording: anything that ensures diary entries are as accurate as possible.

Image-based diaries

Photo and video diaries require clear and informative images, rather than aesthetic or cinematographic excellence, so ask participants to refrain from using filters and effects, or from editing footage. To re-emphasise the point made in the last section, participants mustn't put themselves at risk by trying to photograph people who would rather not be photographed, entering places that are off-limits or other potentially hazardous behaviour. If participants have a contact number to call with any queries or problems that arise while out shooting, this can prevent them getting into difficulties. Gathering video and photo footage is usually an enjoyable method for participants, so ensure it's simple for them to submit their material to enable them to complete the project easily.

Following the process at Figure 4.2, here are some outline ideas on how the example diary studies mentioned might work in practice.

EVENT-BASED DIARY STUDY: UPGRADING LOCAL PLAY FACILITIES

RESEARCH QUESTIONS
What's good and bad about current provision? Does it meet the needs of children and adults?

PARTICIPANTS
Parents and carers who are regular users.

DIARY APPROACH
Event-based: participants could be asked to make an entry each time they visit with their children over the course of a month. This could be a structured written diary (so they can do it in-situ while their children are playing!), with photos to illustrate (of equipment and facilities, not children), with space for any further comments, such as ideas for improvements. The structured questions could cover the state of the facilities and equipment, interactions and note the equipment that their children use most.

ANALYSIS

This will yield mainly quantitative data, so can be analysed for the positives and negatives that are reported most, such as levels of social interaction for children and adults, and use of equipment. The qualitative data in the suggestions for improvements can be categorised to identify themes.

TIME-BASED
DIARY STUDY:
NEIGHBOUR
RELATIONSHIPS
ON ESTATE

RESEARCH QUESTIONS

What is the state of relationships between neighbours? Is there a sense of neighbourly cohesion or isolation? What factors might play a part?

PARTICIPANTS

Residents, chosen randomly from all parts of the estate. Check for a good demographic-cross section of participants and invite any under-represented groups as necessary. A good size sample will allow greater analysis, and allow for a drop-out rate.

DIARY APPROACH

Time-based: participants could be asked to complete the same questions each day, offering insight into the frequency and nature of interactions with neighbours. (If none take place, that's also useful data.) Email, online or written diaries could be used to record interactions for two to three weeks, categorised by duration, type, tone, etc (positive, negative or neutral).

ANALYSIS

This will yield largely quantitative data, allowing analysis of the numbers and types of interactions. If numbers permit, it may be possible to assess whether some areas have more positive or negative interactions, and whether there are factors like design features in common. It may also be possible to see differences in the experiences of different demographic groups.

UNSTRUCTURED
DIARY STUDY:
EFFECTS OF
TOWN CENTRE
DESIGN FOR
PEOPLE WITH
MOBILITY
AND SENSORY
IMPAIRMENTS

RESEARCH QUESTIONS

What issues do people with mobility and sensory impairments encounter in navigating the town centre? What design features help and hinder journeys and access?

PARTICIPANTS

People with a range of impairments, and their carers/partners/parents, if appropriate.

DIARY APPROACH

Unstructured: this gives individuals the freedom to decide what they want to discuss rather than answering pre-set questions which may not reflect their experiences (some prompts might be helpful though). A note of the route, time taken, day/time and purpose will help contextualise the entries. Participants could use photos, video and voice recording to document experiences or record a narrative, with added text if they want to add more detail.

ANALYSIS

Using the 'Quick guide to analysing qualitative data' on p. 60, prepare a coding structure to identify categories within the narratives. Break these down into more specific topics and then cross-reference and rearrange the data to look for other patterns and recurring themes.

4.5   **WORKING WITH DIARY MATERIAL**

Data management

If participants can submit material throughout the study period, review it as it comes in rather than waiting until the dataset is complete. Once the study period is over, the first task is to add all the submitted material to the project data library (there's more detail at section 2.3, p. 21, on this process). Check that all the material is usable and complete; if anything further is needed, request it as soon as possible. Otherwise the data collection phase is now complete, so thank the participants fulsomely, ask for their feedback and any suggestions for improving the process, and whether they would like to be kept informed of progress and future events, in which case add them to the mailing list.

Analysing quantitative material

Structured diaries with standardised questions or multiple-choice answers will generate numerical quantitative data. This should be reasonably straightforward to organise and interpret, using spreadsheets or survey software, and the results can be presented as simple statistics, with supporting graphs or tables; see the 'Quick guide to reporting research' on p. 136 for more detail.

Analysing qualitative material

Depending on the nature of the diaries and the research objectives, one starting point for analysis is to identify patterns within the data, such as regular behaviour or similarities in attitudes. Alternatively, it might be productive to look at themes like journeys, common locations, optional and necessary activities, or tasks that were easy to complete and those that were problematic. Another approach is to cluster material related to each research question and analyse it from there. While it's natural to focus on commonalities, it's just as important to examine the whole spectrum of responses in qualitative analysis. Resist any urge to render qualitative data as statistics. The analysis will often raise further issues for consideration, so it will probably become an iterative process, which should continue until no more insights or queries arise. Refer to the 'Quick guide to analysing qualitative data' on p. 60 for more guidance.

- **Unstructured text-based diaries:** start by reading each submission individually, using the analysis guide drafted at the preparation stage to highlight relevant content. At the same time, note any themes or issues that hadn't been considered before to follow up, particularly if they recur. Always ask participants for clarification, explanation or more detail. Don't try and guess what was meant, or fill in gaps.

- **Image-based diaries**: photographs often need further discussion to bring out their full significance, so it's common after a photo diary exercise for the photographers to review the images as a group. This allows participants to contribute to the analysis phase. They can cluster images into topics or themes, draw comparisons and highlight contrasts, explore different meanings, and discuss their own perceptions and experiences. This gives everyone not just a chance to talk about their photos, but also to see others' perspectives, which can spark ideas and debate such that the pool of images becomes more than the sum of its parts. Participants' discussions add much to the analysis and interpretation processes, but don't replace them; the design/research team still has to do its own analysis, looking for connections with the research questions, and other emerging themes and patterns. Some themes will be more relevant than others, but note them all anyway. Issues that seem insignificant at this stage may appear in a new light later on.

4.6   KEY POINTS SUMMARY

> Text and image-based diary studies provide self-reported information that allows an understanding of people's experiences and attitudes in their natural context, giving researchers a sense of seeing the world through participants' eyes.

Diaries can be structured or unstructured, depending on the purpose of the research and the information required.

Image-based diary-keeping is an accessible and engaging activity for many people and can provide new perspectives on seeing places and communities. However, text-based diaries, which may be handwritten, emailed or completed online, can yield more nuance and detail.

Effective planning, including recruiting sufficient people, piloting the programme, briefing the participants, good communication and technological simplicity are key to a diary project's success.

Diary studies can be biased by participant selection, the information that participants choose to include and exclude, and by interpretation errors in analysis, all of which should be factored into reporting.

Both image and text-based diary studies can produce a lot of qualitative material. An analysis guide and a structured approach will make this task simpler. Note other themes and issues that emerge during initial analysis, and then review with these in mind. This then becomes an iterative process of making connections and seeing patterns between different data clusters.

A QUICK GUIDE TO ANALYSING QUALITATIVE DATA

Data comes in many shapes and forms. Any material with the potential to provide useful knowledge can be treated as data.

Think like a researcher. Consider whether the data is reliable and valid. Be mindful of bias at every stage, and impartial in reviewing, analysing and interpreting the material, and presenting findings.

If some groups views are under-represented or if there's insufficient information to work with, collect more data if possible.

Qualitative data analysis requires a systematic approach, which will usually be an iterative process rather than a linear progression.

The **research objectives and questions** should provide a structure for analysing material. It's then possible to group material relating to each research question and analyse it thematically.

Start the analysis process with the end in mind. What outputs are needed and what's the best way to produce them? This helps gives direction to analysing a large collection of mixed material.

Be open to new issues that weren't in the initial plan and reconsider the objectives if needed.

The analysis will be largely determined by the quantity and nature of the material, and the scope of the research. One of the following processes will suit most projects.

AFFINITY DIAGRAMMING

This visual method of analysing data works well with data consisting of comments from written feedback or conversations. Each comments is summarised on a post-it note (colour-coding can be helpful), which are grouped and regrouped to bring together material on research questions, topics or themes and linkages between these. Each reshuffle develops the analysis, which is recorded and reviewed as the process goes on.

Coding is appropriate for larger or more complex datasets, or where a deeper level of analysis is needed. This is one possible approach.

01 **Review:** with the research questions in mind, go through all the material and note initial perceptions. Listen to interviews, look at photos, watch videos, read documents and become familiar with the data as a whole.

02 **Sort and categorise:** using the research questions to form top-level headings, systematically sort the material into categories (anything that doesn't quite fit can be put aside for now). During this process, highlight words, phrases or themes that recur or seem particularly noteworthy.

03 **Code:** do another pass looking for the main topics and themes within each category, and code the material with tags or keywords. There will be material that relates to more than one topic or theme, which can be regrouped and coded further in the next passes.

04 **Analyse:** go through the topics and themes, and draft a brief initial summary of each one. Look for connections between them, and note anomalies and exceptions as well. See if material that couldn't initially be categorised can now be allocated. Re-sort and regroup the material within the categories, and add any new insights that this reveals to the summaries.

05 Review the summaries for an initial analysis of the data as a whole. Keep re-sorting and regrouping the material using the topics, themes and keywords, adding to the summaries and developing the analysis.

Here's how an initial sort of some material might look with a very small number of sample topics and themes. Each subsequent pass would sort the material differently, grouping by topic, theme and keywords.

Table 4.1

CATEGORIES	PUBLIC REALM	TRANSPORT/ACCESS	DESIGN
TOPICS	Streetscape	Traffic and parking	Materials and finishes
	Open/green space	Cycle routes	Visual quality
	Landscaping and trees	Pedestrian routes	Lighting
THEMES	Feeling welcoming	Reducing car use	Local character
	Improving safety	Accessibility	Sustainability

5 Exhibitions and public meetings

5.1	**INTRODUCTION**

Moving along the participation spectrum to 'inform' and 'consult', exhibitions and meetings are typical first steps in introducing a proposal to the public and consulting on it. They're now increasingly likely to include participative elements to encourage community input, however, rather than just give out information. Continuing to encourage designers to think like researchers, this chapter looks at making the most of these events to gather information and develop ongoing conversations, to maximise their value for everyone.

EXHIBITIONS AND MEETINGS	Methodology type: **qualitative	quantitative**
	Level of participation: **inform/consult**
	Time/resource needed for data collection: **low**
	Time/resource needed for data analysis: **medium**
	Useful for: **understanding site context** **understanding attitudes/perceptions/values/feelings** **testing/getting opinions/feedback**

5.2	**PREPARATION**

Figure 5.1
Suggested process in
exhibitions and meetings

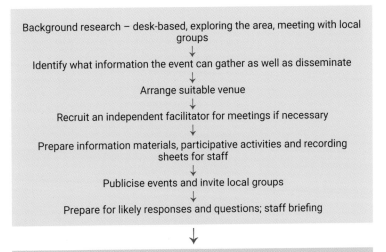

Background research – desk-based, exploring the area, meeting with local groups
↓
Identify what information the event can gather as well as disseminate
↓
Arrange suitable venue
↓
Recruit an independent facilitator for meetings if necessary
↓
Prepare information materials, participative activities and recording sheets for staff
↓
Publicise events and invite local groups
↓
Prepare for likely responses and questions; staff briefing

↓

Hold meeting/exhibition, gather data

↓

Add to data library and back up
↓
Get feedback from participants
↓
Review – analysis – interpretation
↓
Summarise findings/communicate/feed into next phase of design

Listening and learning

There are two prerequisites to a positive ongoing dialogue with the local community:

1. A willingness to listen and learn from them
2. A meaningful understanding of the site context.

This is about more than design and planning issues: it's about appreciating human factors and being open about the proposal's consequences for local people in the

65

immediate and surrounding areas. Practices that show through their approach to public exhibitions and meetings that they have these prerequisites are more likely to be viewed as honest brokers and gain trust from the start. I mentioned in the chapter introduction that exhibitions and meetings should, if possible, include participative elements. These are an important part of the listening and learning process, so consider how these can be incorporated to generate dialogue and feedback, and balance out the top-down informing element. There's more on this under 'Maximising participation' in section 5.3.

There are common foreseeable concerns around any new development. For example, increased traffic, loss of green space, effects on views, environmental degradation, impact on the landscape or historic character, and pressure on local infrastructure and services. It should be possible to anticipate which concerns are likely for any given scheme, so decide how best to address them beforehand. Designers equipped with good background research, who have explored the area to gain a sense of its identity and have chatted with people about local issues from the start, should be well placed to respond to concerned residents. It's vital people feel heard and understood, so let them express their anxieties, listen and show empathy, regardless of your own views.

While concerns may arise from misapprehensions or unclear information, some may be perfectly valid, meaning the proposals need to be revised before concerns harden into objections. This is especially pertinent when the proposals are first revealed.

An example I heard about occurred at a public meeting to introduce proposed new housing on the edge of a former mining village. A resident asked if the architects were aware of the disused mine tunnels beneath the proposed site. Surveys hadn't shown anything, so this was news to the architects. But he had an interest in local mining history, and produced maps showing there were in fact old tunnels on the site. Although those plans had to be scrapped, this was much less costly than if the issue had only come to light once work started on site. So local knowledge can be invaluable.

Selecting a venue

In deciding on a meeting or exhibition venue, be aware of factors that could prevent or deter people from attending an event there. Are there cultural issues (holding a meeting in a pub or a religious building is generally inadvisable) or physical barriers (a venue with no access for wheelchair users, or in a location with no nearby public transport links, for example)? Might an institutional or corporate venue be

Figure 5.2a

Figure 5.2b

Figure 5.2c

intimidating for some? The main thing is that people feel the process is for them and open to them, and the venue should confirm this. Somewhere familiar to many local people, that's culturally neutral, fully accessible and easy to reach, is ideal.

There will be many local residents who can't or won't attend public events, of course, but nobody should miss out, so put all the exhibition or presentation material online with the option to leave feedback or post questions. Consider taking the information to groups who are known to be unlikely to attend public events or access the information online; give presentations to community organisations and display exhibition boards in several different venues to reach a range of groups. Ultimately, the choice of venue for exhibitions or meetings shouldn't exclude anyone, but those who don't attend must be still be able to engage by other means. There's more on this in section 5.3.

Publicising events

The nature of the locale, and the development's scale and potential impact will help decide how best to promote events. The aim is to ensure as many people as possible see publicity for exhibitions or meetings and, more importantly, get to know about the proposal and the changes it could bring. Social media and online promotion will reach a proportion of the local population but proactive contact, face-to-face communication and street publicity are still essential for maximum engagement.

This means initiating contact with demographic groups who are likely to be under-represented at public events. Ask local organisations and local authority officers for advice on community groups to include and how to approach them. Personally inviting marginalised groups to events helps assure them their involvement is welcomed and valued, but remember that outreach, arranging meetings and building relationships can take time, and the more diverse the area, the more time and care are needed to develop these relationships. Ask all new contacts if they would like to be added to the mailing list for project updates; they may choose not to participate at this stage, but may wish to later on, so keep them in the loop.

Put up posters in the streets, shops and public buildings in the vicinity of the site. Better still, have staffed street displays, give leaflets to passers-by, discuss the proposal, listen to their views and offer feedback forms. Street stalls or pop-ups can attract more interest and engagement than public events, and it's good to offer plenty of options for informal discussion. A quick chat while out shopping will suit most people better than giving up an evening to attend a meeting: even more so if there are simple fun activities involved and/or edible treats on offer (see section 6.6, p. 95, for more suggestions on street engagement.) Make the most of local newspapers and distribute leaflets to residents, to commuters at stations in rush hour and to shoppers at supermarkets at peak times. Info-bomb the area by any means necessary, so that nobody can say they were unaware.

Presenting information

When should a meeting be organised, and when is an exhibition better? A public meeting can be more appropriate at the start of a project to introduce a proposal or ideas for a site, as it allows general debate while a range of options are still open. It also helps the team gauge local feeling about the project, which can be useful in developing further participation. An exhibition is often better later in the programme to display detailed designs or a preferred option. In fact, some authorities stipulate that a public exhibition takes place only once a scheme's ready to go to planning. The rationale is that proposals should be discussed thoroughly with relevant local groups first. Then the designers incorporate their feedback through various iterations until most parties are reasonably satisfied, which will have addressed many concerns that the wider public would also have had. Having already ironed out some problems and improved the initial ideas, the proposals are then presented to the community for formal consultation, with potential grounds for objection reduced or removed. This may well be a sensible process to adopt whether officially required or not.

The golden rule for preparing for any public presentation is more images, fewer words. People generally understand a proposal better by seeing it rather than hearing or reading about it, so accessible plans and drawings are essential. They need realistic visualisations of street-level views in proper perspectives (I can't stress this enough) to understand visual impacts and other effects on the immediate area. Lovely renders of idealised locations and beautiful people don't help local residents' understanding or designers' credibility. I'd also like to suggest that less is more when it comes to maps. Provide the basic context but don't inundate people with a mass of topographical detail and survey data.

There are three relatively simple things the design team can do here to build trust and improve communications with the community.

1. **When initially presenting the proposal, stick to the need-to-know information** and the basic overall picture: the nature and scale of the proposed development, the rationale and the potential local consequences. If people are offered a lot of detail at this stage, they can be sidetracked by minor aspects and lose sight of the proposal as a whole (see 'Bikeshedding' in the Appendix on p. 177). Discussions will be more balanced and productive if they start with the general concept and the options available, and allow ideas to develop from there.

2. The second suggestion leads on from this: **take care not to present proposals in a way that implies decisions have already been made**. When detailed plans are presented early on, people are liable to interpret them as saying 'This is what we *will* do', rather than 'This is what we *could* do.' And when they feel that plans have already been decided, they conclude that the process is a tick-box exercise and disengage. Fortunately, there's a simple solution: talk to people first and then start designing.

3. Lastly, **manage expectations from the outset**. Which elements of the development are non-negotiable (due to local plan requirements, for instance) and which are open for discussion and can be decided or at least influenced by the local community? Explain any constraints, whether site issues, budget or contextual factors, so people can take a realistic, informed view.

BIAS ISSUES IN EXHIBITIONS AND MEETINGS

PLANNING

Exclusion bias | Self-selection bias | Selection bias

Is the event equally welcoming and accessible to all or are some groups more likely than others to attend? If so, how can these imbalances be addressed to attract a wide range of attendees?

DATA COLLECTION

Interviewer bias | Procedural bias

Do any practical or logistical factors determine who can attend, such as timing, location and venue? Will presenters or facilitators create a positive first impression

ANALYSIS

Confirmation bias | Observer-expectancy effect

Are those analysing the data making unexpected findings or only seeing what they expected to see?

COMMUNICATION

Curse of Knowledge | Reporting bias

Is the whole range of views represented in reporting an event or mainly the majority? Are nuances, paradoxes and complexities covered or just the easily explained and understood data? And are materials for the public written in language that anyone can understand?

PARTICIPANTS

Anchoring | Base rate fallacy | Bikeshedding | Framing effect | Halo effect | Illusory truth effect | Reactive devaluation

Think about how attendees will process the information presented. Is there a lot of distracting detail? Would people receive information more easily if it were presented in other ways (for example, using videos or infographics instead of text)? Might people's responses to information be coloured by who gives it and how it fits with what they already know?

See the Appendix for explanations of these types of bias.

5.3	RUNNING EXHIBITIONS AND MEETINGS

Maximising participation

An exhibition allows people to take in information in their own time. It may just consist of maps and boards for basic information dissemination or it may feature interactive elements that enable people to give feedback and contribute ideas. This can be simple methods like questionnaires or polls, a suggestions box, adding stickers or colour-coded flags to drawings or maps, or graffiti boards or post-it notes for people to write comments on aspects of the proposal. A little more effort to create, but more engaging for people, is a physical or virtual model of the site with elements that can be added, moved and altered, with staff on hand to engage with participants, listen to their thoughts and note their responses. Whatever the methods, an exhibition needs to present the proposal in ways people can easily understand, showing awareness of its implications for the community and potential positive and negative effects, and offering people the opportunity to contribute ideas and make their views known.

Public meetings can create a sense of engagement and a constructive dialogue between the design team and the community, and don't have to stick to the traditional top-down model of merely informing. Practicalities on the day can make a big difference: catering and room layout in particular. Greeting attendees on the door and offering drinks and snacks makes people feel welcomed and shows their presence is valued. If space permits, a café-style room layout (round tables each seating a few people) creates a more sociable atmosphere than seating in rows, and allows for group discussions and activities: an opportunity often worth taking at this stage. If a question-and-answer session is included, and it certainly should be, the chair or facilitator needs to be able to manage vociferous individuals or groups, so there's time for everyone to have their say and air a range of views.

At any events at the start of a programme, it's worth stressing that it's a long-haul journey rather than a short hop, and encouraging everyone to continue to contribute as the plans develop. Outline the next steps, confirm the extent to which the next iteration of the design will incorporate their feedback, mention how the results of this event will be communicated, and give details about future opportunities for participation. Above all, assure people their views have been listened to and that their input is important.

Communicating

Remember the adage that people may forget what you said but they will remember how you made them feel? Repeat this mantra before all public events. If you can make people feel valued, respected and involved, that feeling will stay with them; they'll feel positive about the process and want to continue to be part of it. The consequences of making them feel unimportant and belittled shouldn't need to be spelled out. Remember that an exciting new project for the design team can be a source of anxiety and concern for local people. I stress that the best thing designers can do is listen. Keep the time spent talking at public events to a minimum; stick to summarising the proposals and resist the urge to discuss design concepts and details, or push the various merits of the scheme. Correct misconceptions or factual inaccuracies by all means, but don't argue with people's views. These are platforms for people to express their opinions, and for those opinions to be heard and noted.

Professionals can easily forget laypeople don't have their expert knowledge and technical insight (see 'Curse of Knowledge' in the Appendix, p. 176). It's a common complaint that when designers present information to the public, it's too technically complex for most to understand, or uses too much unfamiliar language. And this is undoubtedly an effective way to get a relationship with the community off to a difficult start. 'Cognitive ease' and 'cognitive strain' are useful concepts to bear in mind in preparing information for public events (Kahneman, 2011).

Cognitive ease is a positive feeling created by information that's easy to process and that uses familiar concepts. When people experience cognitive ease, they are more likely to respond positively to the information itself, and the higher the level of cognitive ease, the more receptive people are.

The opposite effect is cognitive strain, which happens when information requires too much mental effort to process, perhaps because it's overly complex or badly presented. Cognitive strain not only makes people feel stressed and unhappy, it also arouses feelings of suspicion. The take-away here is that if people can easily understand what you say, they're more likely to trust and believe you; if they don't understand you, they won't trust you. There's no need to dumb down or over-simplify, just aim for a good level of cognitive ease as you prepare information for your audiences.

Facilitating meetings

Effective facilitation involves a lot of work and requires a lot of skill. The facilitator needs to make sure everyone who wants to speak has their say, gets a wide range of views from the group, and keeps the meeting positive and productive. They need to be sensitive to groups and individuals who may find it hard to make their voices heard, be conscious of group dynamics and body language, and have the confidence to quieten over-dominating or disruptive attendees and habitual interrupters – all this while staying on topic and keeping to time. For meetings about large or controversial projects, it's wise to bring in an experienced independent facilitator; smaller or straightforward projects can be handled in-house if – and only if – there are experienced staff available.

Gathering information

By approaching an event in researcher mode rather than as a designer, just standing next to an exhibition board listening to people's opinions can be vital information-gathering (and I emphasise 'listening'). It's helpful to create a simple form for staff to note people's responses, whatever the format of the event. This allows comments made in conversation to be recorded in a consistent way, generating usable material for the project data library. The research objectives and questions can work as headings to categorise comments, along with any initial responses expressed to the proposal (e.g. for/against/undecided), and areas of concern. It's not intended as a questionnaire, just a standard record of any useful information from informal conversations.

Questions and comments from the audience at meetings should definitely be recorded; an audio recording is usually the best option but a capable note-taker will suffice. This is useful material for the data library, not only for insights to local concerns and issues but also to inform future communications, showing that you're listening. If any participative activities are included, this will generate still more material in the form of models, maps, post-it notes on flipcharts or feedback forms.

Finally, some equally important information to collect is attendees' feedback on the event itself and their perceptions of the process so far. A brief email evaluation form sent shortly after, and/or a paper-based one on the day will give at least a rough indication of how well messages were communicated and understood, and whether the process is being conducted effectively. Take advantage of the chance to grow the mailing list too, and encourage attendees to give their email addresses to receive news and updates.

5.4	WORKING WITH MATERIAL FROM EXHIBITIONS AND MEETINGS

Review

Exhibitions and meetings will generate a mixture of types of material. There will be quantitative material, such as completed questionnaires, feedback forms, records of interactions with attendees with categorised responses and attendance figures. There may also be a mass of qualitative material, such as marked-up drawings, diagrams on flipcharts, photographs and notes from conversations. Before starting any analysis, the first task is to add it all to the project data library. The 'Quick guide to analysing qualitative data' on p. 60 sets out the essentials on working with qualitative material and should be helpful in giving overall direction to the analysis and interpretation phase.

Analysis

This material will probably serve a number of purposes, including forming the basis of a report back to participants and/or the client, shaping the development process and informing decision-making. Beginning the analysis and interpretation with the end in mind can help give a greater clarity of purpose to the proceedings:

- What are the final products that are required?
- Who are the audiences?
- What are their information needs?
- What is the best way to fulfil those?

Figure 5.4
Feedback cards are one way to add an interactive element to exhibitions and meetings

There will be plenty of quantitative material from feedback forms, online responses and conversations. This material needs to be expressed statistically, showing initial trends in favour or against the proposal, or views on more specific matters, for example. Check the 'Quick guide to reporting research' on p. 136 for advice on analysing and presenting this kind of information. Exhibitions and meetings will generate qualitative content as well from participative activities and conversations. The 'Quick guide to analysing qualitative data' on p. 60 suggests steps for turning this into analysable material and bringing out the full value of participants' input.

Dissemination

Producing a publicly available summary of an event is always a good idea – the sooner after the event, the better – describing the attendance, the range of responses and queries, and giving details of next steps and further opportunities to contribute. A report on the event, articles in the local press, a newsletter, a dedicated website, social media or a liaison group for bigger projects can all facilitate this. It's also worth giving details of named contacts who can respond to queries.

People can become disheartened and lose interest if there appears to be no response to their contributions, no matter how much activity might be going on behind the scenes. Ongoing communication helps stimulate discussion and maintain engagement, so it's important to provide regular updates, even if there's no major news. The key is to keep communication channels open and ensure participants have a sense that their input is welcomed as the project develops. The 'Quick guide to reporting research' gives further guidance on communicating findings and key messages.

5.5	KEY POINTS SUMMARY

> Exhibitions and meetings tend to focus on disseminating information, so complement them with more participatory activities to start gathering feedback and suggestions.
>
> Don't present a lot of detailed information or proposals that appear to have been decided already.
>
> Give people plenty of opportunity to offer their views and make sure they feel listened to.
>
> Research the area and its residents thoroughly beforehand and make the most of local knowledge from the outset.
>
> Do everything possible to ensure everyone affected by the development gets to see something about it. Be proactive in making contact and use all available communication channels.
>
> Use clear and unambiguous language, avoiding jargon, design-speak and technical terminology.
>
> Record meetings and take notes of conversations and the themes that emerged; they can be a valuable source of information as the project develops.
>
> Produce a report back on the event, along with information on next steps, further opportunities for contributing and named contacts – and keep communication channels open.

Do good desk research. Understanding the socio-economic context and the level of interest in the site will get discussions off to a good start.

Maintain a contacts database of community and amenity groups, civic societies, campaigning organisations, tenants' and residents' associations, councillors and other key local figures and bodies, and ensure they're invited to events. Assess what the **main issues and areas of local concern** are likely to be and how to respond. Look at responses to previous planning applications and scan the local press to see what's likely to attract support or objections.

Check for any other engagement programmes running at the same time to avoid clashes or consultation fatigue.

Make sure that everyone who needs to hear about the proposed development does. Everyone affected should know about the proposal and how to register their views.

Consider a separate consultation zone for residents or businesses in the immediate vicinity of the site, and make personal contact to offer individual discussions with those potentially most affected.

Hold an exhibition or an event in a few different places rather than just one, if possible.

Accept that **people get involved in consultations for a wide range of reasons,** driven by many different agendas and motivations, and various levels of investment in the process.

Create a basic form for staff to note conversations they have with people. The format depends on the nature of the exercise, but as a minimum include whether it's a comment, suggestion or query; the aspect of the proposal concerned; whether it's for information, action or reply; whether it was from a resident, business or organisation.

Pilot, rehearse, refine and re-test activities and resources for any event.

ON THE DAY

Think like a researcher. Identify what kind of material the event can contribute to the research objectives and how to capture it.

Ensure there are enough **staff** on hand, and that they're visibly identifiable.

Staff are there to listen, take notes and answer questions, not to extol the merits of the proposal.

Aim for 'cognitive ease'; communicate using concepts and illustrations that people are comfortable with. Refer to the familiar, well-known and tangible, and avoid technical language and design jargon.

Look at who attends and who doesn't; consider the extent to which local groups are over- or under-represented, and whose voices are being heard.

Every event is an opportunity to grow the mailing list, so encourage people to sign up to receive email updates.

Collect anonymous feedback from participants (a short paper-based questionnaire is best) to gauge how well messages were communicated and understood, how people are feeling about the project and the participation process, and any comments or suggestions for future events.

Publish a summary of any public event. Sooner rather than later is best, with a quick round-up of numbers involved, what took place, some photos and next steps.

Desire Lines: A Guide to Community Participation in Designing Places

6   Survey methods

'99% of all statistics only tell 49% of the story.'

–Ron DeLegge II

6.1	INTRODUCTION

This chapter offers some golden rules and detailed guidance on getting the most from surveys. The main reason to run a survey is to produce statistics. This normally entails gathering data with questionnaires, but can also include polls, votes or any exercise where people answer standardised questions en masse and their responses are aggregated. If people have good questions to answer, and if they answer truthfully, surveys can provide large amounts of valuable information. These are two big 'ifs', of course, as detailed in section 6.2.

It looks at some advantages of surveys, along with some pitfalls to avoid. It discusses questionnaire design in detail, and some alternative survey approaches, before looking at analysing and reporting the data to produce evidence-based insight to inform decision-making and design.

SURVEYS

Methodology type:
quantitative

Level of participation:
consult

Time/resource needed for data collection:
low

Time/resource needed for data analysis:
medium

Useful for:
understanding site context
understanding attitudes/perceptions/values/feelings
testing/getting opinions/feedback

| 6.2 | SURVEY-BASED APPROACHES |

Advantages of surveys

The great advantage of survey methods is economy of scale. They're a quick, cost-effective way of gathering large amounts of information and generating usable knowledge, particularly on attitudes and behaviour, including:

- **Investigating** perceptions and opinions across large numbers of people.
- **Discovering** common patterns within groups.
- **Comparing** differences between groups.
- **Gathering** baseline data to assess subsequent trends or changes.
- **Enabling** generalisations, when sample size permits.

This versatility makes surveys a useful method throughout the design process, from identifying relevant issues at the outset to getting feedback on options, through to post-completion evaluation. They're a familiar format for most participants, and it's reasonably simple to create and run a survey with the user-friendly software available. Packages normally include calculation and analysis features, so statistical ability isn't required either.

Disadvantages of surveys

Surveys, methodologically speaking, aren't quite as straightforward to design as they may seem. It's very easy for the questions, answer options or structure to unwittingly skew the results. I note these pitfalls not to dissuade anyone from running surveys but as a reminder that flawed surveys yield flawed information, which no one wants.

Firstly, opportunities for bias abound (see the boxed text at the end of section 6.3). Surveys rely on self-report, asking respondents to tick the box that best describes their behaviour or attitudes. However, respondents may also give what they think are correct or desirable answers; they may interpret questions in unforeseen ways, or they may under-or over-state their attitudes or behaviour. They might find the questionnaire dull and stop considering their answers carefully, or it might not include the questions or answer options they want. But their responses must still be accepted at face value.

Secondly, can the complexity of human experience and behaviour really be captured in simple answers to simple questions? A survey works fine for uncontroversial or uncomplicated topics, but not when nuanced or in-depth information is needed.

And I'm afraid there's more. Do the findings represent the views of the silent majority who didn't complete the questionnaire? Surveys can reflect what people usually do or prefer, but are less effective at finding out why. Behaviour and feelings may also change over time, so a dataset is a snapshot of a specific moment but has a limited shelf life, especially so in a design context where attitudes towards a proposal will often change as it develops. Don't let this put you off using surveys; they can yield highly valuable data, but careful construction and testing beforehand are essential.

6.3	**PREPARATION**

There's only one shot at a survey so it needs to be right first time. This means that preparation is vital, with thorough questionnaire testing and review before the survey goes live, and making sure it reaches all the target demographics: see Figure 6.1 for a suggested survey process. Double-check at the outset that survey responses will be stored securely, especially if participants' personal details are included. And beware of consultation fatigue; make sure there are no other local consultations running at around the same time.

Sampling

The sampling strategy, in research terms, is the method of choosing participants for a project out of all the potential participants. In spatial design, the nature of the proposal and its context can determine the sampling strategy. Sometimes it's possible to engage with all those potentially affected by a development – every household in a street, for example – so the strategy might aim for a 100% sample. But when this isn't practicable, how to decide who participates? For a public realm proposal, the sampling strategy might focus on maximising the participation of specific groups or achieving a minimum number of responses. Is it likely that survey participants' responses might vary according to demographic factors, postcode area and so on? If so, survey enough people to yield usable data and allow valid comparisons between groups. And if the initial survey doesn't receive many responses from certain groups, get more responses from people in those groups until there's enough to work with. Be prepared to make direct contact and offer active encouragement to marginalised groups to ensure they have their say. Remember that for survey results to have any reliability, groups whose views may differ from the majority must be included, and the extent of those differences understood. (This might mean a follow-up meeting or focus group, for example.)

Figure 6.1
Suggested survey process

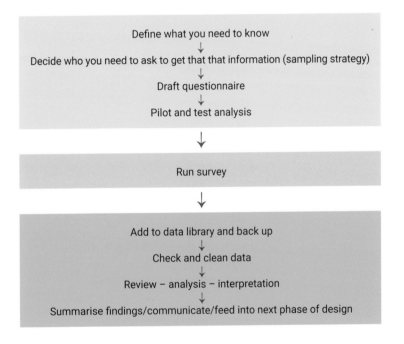

Define what you need to know
↓
Decide who you need to ask to get that that information (sampling strategy)
↓
Draft questionnaire
↓
Pilot and test analysis

↓

Run survey

↓

Add to data library and back up
↓
Check and clean data
↓
Review – analysis – interpretation
↓
Summarise findings/communicate/feed into next phase of design

Piloting

The piloting phase is perhaps the most critical part of the survey process. Don't even think about launching a questionnaire without testing it first on colleagues, friends, community contacts and anyone with a few minutes to spare.

Piloting has three purposes:

1. Identifying technical issues in completing the questionnaire.
2. Checking whether the questions and answers are clear, and follow a logical structure.
3. Noting the time needed for completion (normally longer than expected!)

Keep fine-tuning the questions and re-testing until no further improvements can be made. If there are questions with an 'Other, please specify' option, check for frequently occurring responses there that could be added to the multiple-choice options; also check whether free-text responses will be analysable (a word limit or different question wording might be necessary, for instance). Before going live, double-check that printed questionnaires are identical to the final online version, to ensure consistency when these responses are input manually.

Test analysis

Run some test reports on the pilot responses and/or some dummy data, and make sure that data appears in the correct format and fields, that it can be sorted, filtered and analysed to the required level of detail, and does everything else needed. Finally, ask the pilot respondents for honest feedback on the experience of completing the survey. Was it repetitive? Was it engaging? Were the answer options adequate? Did they feel there were any leading questions?

And on the subject of bias, the pilot phase is the last chance to decide whether the questions are actually going to generate the information required. Is anything missing? Are the issues relevant to the people who will be responding? Does the survey reflect their concerns and interests, or that of the design team's? (Hint: it should be theirs, as far as possible.)

BIAS ISSUES IN
SURVEYS

PLANNING
Exclusion bias | Non-response bias | Self-selection bias | Selection bias
Whether a survey sample is self-selecting or invited, consider whether it will yield enough responses and give a sufficiently representative range of views.

DATA COLLECTION
Attrition bias | Procedural bias | Question-order bias
Might the data be affected by any logistical or practical factors, such as the user-friendliness of an online platform, the time period allowed for completion, or the time when it's being run? Pay close attention to question wording and order, as these can significantly affect responses.

ANALYSIS
Clustering illusion | Confirmation bias | Focusing effect | Illusory correlation | Observer-expectancy effect
Quantitative data allows less scope for subjective interpretation, but can still be misinterpreted. Has undue weight been given to some data? Can connections and correlations be substantiated? Does qualitative data show new insights or is the analysis only finding what was expected? Are any groups over- or under-represented?

COMMUNICATION
Reporting bias
Does reporting on the data show the full range of views or just the majority view and main trends? Is the reporting objective, covering all aspects of the findings, or does it emphasise certain results more than others?

PARTICIPANTS
Acquiescence bias | Habituation bias | Recall bias | Serial position effect | Social desirability effect | Sponsorship bias
Survey responses can only be taken at face value and their true validity can't be known. Participants' answers can be influenced by whether they are bored or engaged, whether the questions are easy to understand and answer or not, and who is conducting the survey, amongst other factors.

See the Appendix for explanations of these types of bias.

| 6.4 | **QUESTIONNAIRE DESIGN** |

It's easy to design a questionnaire. And it's easy to get it wrong, so much so that this whole section is devoted to avoiding this. Wording and layout influence response rates more than any other factors, so these have to be right. Furthermore, the phrasing of questions and the answer options offered can bias the data without ever becoming apparent. So surveys offer a great way to end up with unreliable findings. To yield good information, a questionnaire needs three things: a good structure, good questions, and good answer options.

People quickly lose interest if they have to complete a lot of personal details, don't get enough chance to express their opinions, are asked boring or irrelevant questions, or if the questionnaire takes too long to complete (anything more than about 15 minutes, for most people). Make sure they're fully engaged all the way to the 'Submit' button.

Good structure

A logical questionnaire flow helps respondents comprehend questions more readily and answer more easily. Start with a short introduction explaining the survey's purpose, who it's for, approximate completion time (noted at the pilot stage) and guidance on completion (if questions can be skipped, or if it can be saved to finish later, for instance). The opening questions should be quick and easy for respondents to answer and put them at ease, and usually ask for factual details like age, gender, location or other necessary personal information.

Use the research strategy questions to develop the body of the questionnaire. Identify the main areas to cover, resisting the temptation to include as many subjects as possible, and refine these into no more than five topics. Then adopt the 'funnelling' technique to arrange the topics, putting the more straightforward ones at the start and proceeding to the more challenging. Briefly introduce the topic at the start of each section, as though changing the subject in conversation. Some questions may need routing (for example 'If "No", please go to Question 4'), but do this only when really necessary, to avoid potential confusion. Close the questionnaire with an 'Any other comments' field, some final thanks, information about next steps and further opportunities for participation, and contact details in case of any queries. Figure 6.2 illustrates the suggested structure.

Figure 6.2
Suggested questionnaire
structure

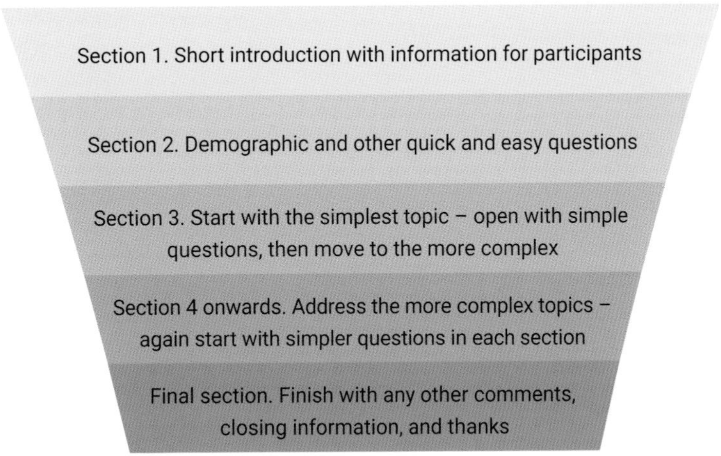

Section 1. Short introduction with information for participants

Section 2. Demographic and other quick and easy questions

Section 3. Start with the simplest topic – open with simple questions, then move to the more complex

Section 4 onwards. Address the more complex topics – again start with simpler questions in each section

Final section. Finish with any other comments, closing information, and thanks

Good questions

Having set the topic structure, decide the issues to cover within each topic, and translate these into good questions that will yield the information required, as shown in Figure 6.3. Questions should be closed whenever possible. Funnelling again, start with general questions within each topic section before moving on to specifics. It's also best to ask about behaviour before moving on to attitudes.

Good questions:
- are asked in neutral terms that don't influence the respondent or imply a preferred answer; for example, 'What's your view of X?' rather than 'Are you in favour of X?'
- are short, simple, jargon-free and phrased in a natural conversational tone
- are unambiguously worded, so respondents are unlikely to misinterpret them
- use specific measures, rather than relative terms like 'several' or 'sometimes'
- ask about one thing at a time
- use concepts and language that will be familiar to respondents, explaining anything that may be unfamiliar
- cover subjects that respondents are likely to know about or have an opinion on
- seek views on a range of alternatives where they exist, rather than asking only about a single/preferred option. ('Which of these features would you prefer?...' rather than 'Would you like X?').

On some issues, some answers can be considered more socially desirable or acceptable than others. These areas may be best approached indirectly; rather

91

than asking for a view straight out, start a question with, for example, 'Some people think X …' or 'People sometimes believe that Y … To what extent does that reflect your view?' Likewise, it can be better to gently broach sensitive topics, with questions like 'Have you seen or heard anything lately about X?'

With the main body of questions drafted, then − and only then − decide what demographic information to ask for. This should be details with direct relevance to the research objectives, which are specifically required. If age or household income information is needed, provide age groups or income bands to select from. Anonymised questionnaires yield more honest answers, so ask for names and contact details only if necessary, or make this optional. Either way, exclude them from the dataset used for analysis, so that responses can't be traced to individuals.

Figure 6.3
Deciding questions

Identify the main broad areas that the questionnaire should cover, based on the research questions
↓
Distil these into a maximum of five topics
↓
Decide the essential aspects that need to be covered within each topic
↓
Turn these into good questions that will yield good data
↓
Add any demographic questions that are needed

Good answers

Good answer options give respondents a meaningful and comprehensive but concise selection of response options. Always offer an equal number of positive and negative response options; an unbalanced spread biases the results. Questions generally require a neutral option ('Don't know', 'Undecided' or 'Neither', for example). These and no answer are valid responses, and are still informative. Deploy open questions and 'Further comments' free-text boxes sparingly (three's considered the maximum) as they take more time to complete and analyse. If there are more than three, look at reconfiguring them as closed questions or incorporating them into another stage of the research where qualitative data is gathered, such a focus group or workshop.

There are many different ways to offer answers to questions about opinions or behaviour. Participants find questionnaires more engaging if answer formats vary, and they may then consider the questions more carefully. So include a variety if possible. See p. 93 for a selection of common answer formats to choose from.

Multiple choice: respondents select one answer from a list of options. Include an 'Other, please specify' option if an exhaustive list of possible responses isn't feasible.

Example: Which of these features would you most like to see on the estate?

☐ Community garden ☐ Bike storage ☐ Play area

☐ More lighting ☐ More trees ☐ More seating

☐ Other, please specify...

Checklist: respondents select all the answers that apply, or a specific number of items (for example, top three) from a list. People won't read to the end of a long list, so about 10–12 items is the maximum.

Example: Which are the three features you would most like to see on the estate?

☐ Community garden ☐ Bike storage ☐ Play area

☐ More lighting ☐ More trees ☐ More seating

☐ Other, please specify...

Ranking: respondents list items in a specified order, for example, order of importance, priority or preference.

Example: Please rate these possible new features in order of preference, with 1 as the one you'd like most:

☐ Community garden ☐ Bike storage ☐ Play area

☐ More lighting ☐ More trees ☐ More seating

☐ Other, please specify...

Attitude measurement scales: these gather information where answers range across a spectrum, such as strength of feeling about a subject or frequency of activity. Some common scales are:

Likert scale: probably the most familiar format, widely used for measuring attitudes. Respondents select from a scale ranging from, for example, 'Strongly agree' to 'Strongly disagree'. Symbols like smiley or sad faces can replace text, if this suits the audience better. Always offer an equal number of options on both sides and a neutral midpoint option.

Example: It would be good to have a community garden on the estate:

☐ Strongly agree ☐ Slightly agree ☐ No opinion ☐ Slightly disagree ☐ Strongly disagree

Continued on next page

Numerical scale: another very common attitude scale, for example, 'What is your level of concern about X, on a scale of 0–10?' This scale also needs an odd number of answer options to allow a neutral choice.

Example: What's your perception of levels of antisocial behaviour on the estate, on a scale of 0-10, where 0 is 'None' and 10 is 'Very high'?

Behavioural scale: respondents report their past and/or likely future behaviour, for instance 'How often do you visit X?' Select from

☐ Every day ☐ Once every week or two

☐ Once a month ☐ Less often

☐ Never.

Example: If there was a community garden on the estate, would you consider getting involved in looking after it?

☐ Definitely would Probably would ☐ Don't know

☐ Probably wouldn't ☐ Definitely wouldn't

Semantic differentiation scale: paired opposites of adjectives are presented at ends of a spectrum, and respondents mark where their view or response lies.

Example:

The estate feels: Safe . . . . .Unsafe

The estate feels: Friendly . . . . Unfriendly

Constant sum scale: respondents distribute 100 points (or pounds, or any other unit of measurement) across a number of categories according to their preferences; they can allocate their points to as few or as many categories as they wish, and decide the number of points to allocate (the calculations need to be made automatically for accuracy). Useful for a more in-depth understanding of priorities.

Example: You have 100 points to divide between the features you'd most like to see on the estate. You can give all the points to one feature, or share them out. Give the most points to features that are most important to you. You have to use all 100 points.

☐ Community garden ☐ Bike storage ☐ Play area

☐ More lighting ☐ More trees ☐ More seating

☐ Other, please specify. ☐ **Total**

6.5   RUNNING SURVEYS

So the questionnaire is honed and tested to perfection. Now it needs to be launched, via as many communication channels as possible. If households in the immediate vicinity of the proposed development could be especially affected, consider door knocking; approach local businesses in person too. A presence at local events and out on the streets, close to the site and/or at busy places, with fliers to give out, can also be good ways to publicise the survey, discuss the issues with people and boost response rates.

Make sure participants have easy access to relevant background information, such as plans, explanatory documents, images, visualisations, maps and videos; surveys have much more value when they reflect informed opinions. Participants will often want to see the results, so add a sign-up for the mailing list. Include a reassurance that data will be held securely and won't be passed to any third party, particularly if personal details are included or if the development's contentious for any reason. In the interests of building trust, be transparent about who's collecting the information for whom, and for what purpose; this can affect how people respond to questions (see 'Sponsorship bias' in the Appendix, on p. 179).

6.6   ALTERNATIVE SURVEY METHODS

Who says surveys have to mean questionnaires? There are lots of ways to get people to share their views without ticking boxes. With some imagination, creativity and enthusiasm for interacting with people in their everyday locations, alternative survey approaches can be more engaging for participants and may yield insights that a standard questionnaire format won't. These aren't suitable methods for in-depth investigation or more sensitive topics, but can be a good way to raise the profile of the engagement programme, taking it to where people are and starting a dialogue. This is essential in areas with communities who are less likely or able to participate in standard consultation processes. These methods could be:

- **Site-specific events referencing the locality.** For example, at a seaside location putting out deckchairs and inviting people to sit and write a postcard about the area.
- **Pop-ups and mobile street stalls.** These could offer survey cards and suggestion boxes, and/or graffiti boards and post-it notes. Alternatively, offer small chalkboards or whiteboards for participants to answer a question on and then photograph them (which also provides demographic context).
- **Food carts.** Offering a free drink or an edible treat in exchange for answers to some questions gets good response rates from all groups, and also communicates a sense of valuing the community.
- **Walks.** Arrange group walkabouts, or a short self-guided walking route with a set of questions or topics to respond to.
- **Photos.** Give picture frames to participants and ask them to photograph (or take selfies of) local features that they like or would like to improve: a good way to engage young people and people for whom language or literacy might be a barrier to giving written responses.

There are now increasing numbers of sophisticated online platforms offering suites of participation methods suitable (although not designed exclusively for) spatial design projects, with features like polls, forums, presentations, live chat, live video, interactive maps and virtual site visits. The rapid take-up by local authorities, practices and clients undoubtedly shows a desire to explore new forms of participation. Nonetheless, asking lots of people the same questions, then aggregating, analysing and reporting the results is essentially a survey process whether the interface is a pop-up street stall, a basic questionnaire or high-tech participation software.

6.7	WORKING WITH SURVEY DATA

The first thing to do once the survey period has ended is to log the batch of survey responses in the data library. The second thing is to clean the data, removing duplicate or unusable responses, correcting any obvious typing mistakes that could affect the analysis, deleting responses to questions that should have been skipped, and any other preparation to ensure the data is error-free and analysable. If paper-based questionnaires were completed, remember to add these responses manually to the rest of the data.

Figures 6.7-10:
Surveys don't have to
mean questionnaires

Checking the data

There are some checks that are worth performing before beginning any analytical work.

Firstly, look at the response rate. How does the number of potential respondents (if known) compare with the number of completed questionnaires? The number of completed responses compared to total number of survey website visitors can be also interesting. There's no standard definition of a 'good' response rate; it depends partly on the nature of the community surveyed. A low rate might still be representative in a more homogenous neighbourhood, whereas a higher rate will be preferable somewhere that a diverse range of views is likely.

Secondly, in a larger scale survey, check how far responses reflect local demographics, if possible. Are any groups especially over- or under-represented? If so, this needs to be borne in mind at the reporting stage, and it might be necessary to invite some groups directly to submit their views for more representative findings. The demographic breakdown of respondents will never precisely mirror the local population, but try and identify any major imbalances before drawing conclusions from the data.

Finally, check to see how many respondents dropped out of the questionnaire, and where; it reflects on the questionnaire design. A high drop-out rate can indicate that a questionnaire was too long, boring, difficult to understand or didn't ask relevant questions. If participation isn't pitched at the right level or capturing people's interest, this should be addressed before the process goes much further.

Analysing the data

Queries and reports can be run now. Any survey software will offer some analytical functionality, but it may be preferable to import the data into a spreadsheet to work on. There will be a mass of numerical data, and if open-ended questions were included, there will be text-based answers to analyse as well. Starting with the number crunching, keep this aspect of the analysis simple, unless a stats expert is available. Identify the obvious headline figures, such as strong majority views or trends, for instance, and also issues where opinion is clearly divided. Where there are no strong signals from the responses, it's enough to note that the data is inconclusive.

If a good cross-section of the community has responded in sufficient numbers, the data may allow comparison between groups: looking at responses according to postcode or demographics, for instance. Small samples don't allow valid comparisons, and neither do responses from groups of fewer than ten within the dataset. But if the data permits, check whether responses from specific groups differ much from the whole and report any significant variations; it's important that the majority view isn't perceived as representative of the whole community. Remember that comparisons between percentage figures need careful wording to avoid misunderstandings. For example, if 30% of respondents want Option A and 60% want Option B, this is often mistakenly expressed as '30% more people preferred Option B to Option A', when in fact 100% more – twice as many – preferred Option B. Also remember to be clear that figures refer to the percentage of those who responded to that question, which may or may not be many of the total respondents, or a representative sample overall; see 'How to lie (unintentionally) with statistics' at section 9.2 for a real-world example.

Analysing free-text responses requires a different approach. If answers to the 'Other' option in multiple-choice questions are short and simple, it might be possible to treat them as quantitative data that can be roughly grouped and counted (an exception to my general advice not to render qualitative data as statistics). Longer and more detailed responses to open-ended questions require the most work. It may be that the research objectives can provide a structure for categorising these initially. It's likely more detailed work will be needed, however, depending on the volume and length of responses. Methodical approaches are set out in the 'Quick guide to analysing qualitative data' on p. 60, which looks for themes and connections in the responses, grouping and regrouping the data in different ways to make sense of it as a whole. In analysing free-text responses, be open to any unexpected issues that seem significant and note them in the analysis even if they weren't in the initial strategy.

The design team, respondents and the client will often find a one-page summary of the headline figures helpful, covering findings on key issues and other significant results. Graphs, charts and infographics make research results more intelligible to many people, so include plenty of illustrations. Be transparent in reporting the results and represent the whole range of views, not just the majority or those who support the proposal. The purpose is to inform the design and work with the public response, so be open about the feedback received. Check the 'Quick guide to reporting research' on p. 136 for more guidance on presenting findings and messages.

6.8 KEY POINTS SUMMARY

> Surveys are a reliable method of collecting data on a mass scale and straightforward for most people to engage with.

Questionnaire design needs careful handling and constant alertness to the possibility of bias.

Clear wording and layout, neutrality and asking only essential questions are key to a good questionnaire.

Include a variety of answer formats to make the questionnaire more engaging for respondents.

Ensure that as many people as possible get the opportunity to respond and make direct contact with those who might not participate to ensure their views are included.

Thorough piloting, review and fine-tuning are essential before a survey goes live; there's only one chance to get it right.

Clean and prepare the data before starting analysis, and check for representativeness and balance. It may be necessary to obtain more responses from some groups before a meaningful analysis can be undertaken.

Look for any significant differences in opinion or experience between specific groups and the overall majority.

Desire Lines: A Guide to Community Participation in Designing Places

7 Focus groups

'To hear, one must be silent.'

–Ursula K. Le Guin

7.1	INTRODUCTION

Still at the 'consult' point of the spectrum, focus groups are a versatile and effective means of gaining insight into people's opinions, feelings, preferences and experiences. The group dynamic is key; it gives participants the opportunity to see matters in new ways, hear different perspectives and discuss challenging questions. The aim is to encourage group responses more than individual viewpoints, and the facilitator's role is vital in maximising participants' involvement to yield good material. This chapter looks at setting aims and structure for focus group sessions, some practical and interpersonal issues to consider, running a group, and collecting, managing and analysing material.

FOCUS GROUPS

Methodology type:
qualitative

Level of participation:
consult

Time/resource needed for data collection:
medium

Time/resource needed for data analysis:
high

Useful for:
understanding site context
understanding attitudes/perceptions/values/feelings
testing/getting opinions/feedback
understanding behaviour/interactions/use of space
site planning/generating ideas
design development

7.2	**FOCUS GROUP RESEARCH**

Focus groups differ from the other group activities covered in these pages, in that the design team selects the participants. Whether to provide variety, balance or homogeneity, participants are chosen for a reason. (A group discussion open to anyone isn't a focus group.) Focus groups are relatively inexpensive and simple to run, and the format suits a wide range of types of participants and topics. At the start of a project, less structured focus groups allow participants to set the agenda and discuss the issues that matter to them, which provides information that designers can use straight away. Further on in the design process, a more structured format can gather feedback on the work in progress and responses to design options.

For participants, focus groups are an opportunity to express themselves on their own terms and in their own words. Questions are mainly open-ended, and the relatively natural, conversational format means that sessions can (and should) be enjoyable for participants. Of course, not everyone feels comfortable talking to a group of strangers and there will always be participants who are less forthcoming; feeling they lack the knowledge or vocabulary to contribute, or nervous about disagreeing with majority views or dominant group members, for example. However, these dynamics can be managed by an experienced facilitator.

There's no doubt that the facilitator's ability is a significant factor in the success of a focus group. Getting maximum yield from the session requires considerable skill. Good listening and observation skills are vital, including for example, the ability to concentrate on what's being said and not being said, picking up on verbal and non-verbal cues, probing, asking for details and explanations, and observing participants' reactions during discussions.

Interpersonal skills are equally important to put everyone at ease and manage any tensions. Furthermore, the facilitator also needs a good understanding of the issues under consideration, as well as to be able to pick up on potentially significant matters that weren't included in the prepared topic schedule. Recalling the impartiality ethic (see section 2.2) the facilitator must maintain a neutral position in discussions, and keep their feelings and opinions to themselves. On this basis, my advice is to use independent facilitators, rather than have staff running focus groups on projects in which they are involved.

7.3	PREPARATION

Figure 7.1
Suggested focus group process

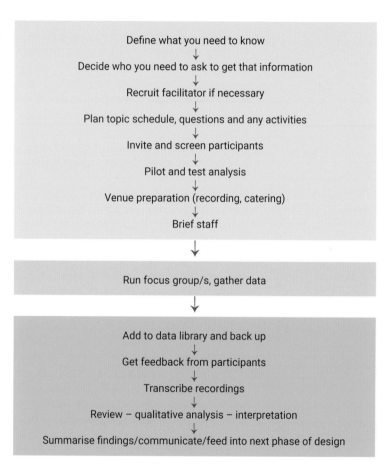

Define what you need to know
↓
Decide who you need to ask to get that information
↓
Recruit facilitator if necessary
↓
Plan topic schedule, questions and any activities
↓
Invite and screen participants
↓
Pilot and test analysis
↓
Venue preparation (recording, catering)
↓
Brief staff

↓

Run focus group/s, gather data

↓

Add to data library and back up
↓
Get feedback from participants
↓
Transcribe recordings
↓
Review – qualitative analysis – interpretation
↓
Summarise findings/communicate/feed into next phase of design

Aims and structure

Before working out the who, where, when and how of setting up a focus group, start with the why. Its purpose must be clear. What is it meant to achieve? What are the questions that need answers? Figure 7.1 suggests a process for preparing and running a focus group. Whether using a structured format or not, prepare a list of topics to guide the session. Less is more; covering a few key topics in depth will yield better information than squeezing lots of issues into the time available. Having said that, the group make-up can play a part here. Homogenous groups can get through a list of topics quicker, as there tends to be greater consensus, whereas more mixed groups usually have a wider range of views and more potential for debate. So take these factors into account in working out what to cover in the session.

If several focus groups are planned, consider the level of question standardisation between them. Asking the same questions in each session means the material can be aggregated, but it can reduce the scope to pursue other interesting topics. Another option is a rolling question schedule. Participants discuss a set of topics in the first session, then issues arising from that session are brought to the second session, then the third session includes new topics that arose in the second, and so on. Although it allows less comparison between sessions, the groups will be able to cover more issues and generate more material (this may not necessarily be seen as an advantage at the analysis stage however!).

Using the funnelling technique described at section 6.4, start a session with general and easily answered questions and get everyone to contribute; then address more challenging topics. It's sensible to cover the most important issues relatively early on while participants are still fresh and there's plenty of time. When presenting information about the proposal, remember that participants may be unused to discussing planning and design issues in depth, so explain any terminology that might be unfamiliar, use everyday concepts and vocabulary, and keep checking for understanding. Discussing controversial or emotionally charged topics can be strenuous for participants, so this should also be factored into the schedule and followed by a break or a more enjoyable activity. Allow about 90 minutes maximum for the session overall.

Aim to gather information about participants' experiences, opinions, feelings and preferences, with a good amount of content in each category. This means asking lots of open-ended questions, starting with, 'What's your experience of ...', 'What do you think about ...' or 'How would you feel if ...', for example. Ensure that questions are relevant to the group, that everyone will understand and will be able to answer them, and remember to ask follow-up questions for more details or explanations: 'Why do you say that?', 'Could you say a bit more about what happened?' And a question that's always worth asking: 'Does anyone have a different view?'

Selecting participants

Having drafted a workable session strategy and time plan, the next step is to put together a good group of people to answer the questions. Send a short screening survey to prospective participants first, explaining the objectives and gathering some details to help select the people who can most usefully contribute. Also include information about recording the session, confidentiality, details of the time and venue, accessibility, length of the session and what will be covered, and check they're happy with these arrangements.

Normally the optimum group size is eight to twelve, although homogenous groups can work with slightly fewer or more than this. The group composition depends on the research objectives. Demographically similar groups will be needed for some issues, but a general mix is suitable when a broad range of perspectives is wanted. Demographic factors play a part in group dynamics, which in turn affects the responses offered. For instance, it's been shown that men tend to dominate discussions in mixed-gender focus groups (Stewart and Shamdasani, 2014), something for the facilitator to monitor.

Venue

Choose a venue that's fully accessible, that everyone can easily reach and where everyone will feel comfortable. Quiet and privacy are essential, so there are no interruptions or distracting background noise. Focus groups are more focused in rooms with natural light. Room size and layout also affect interactions, as people are more relaxed and forthcoming when they have a good amount of personal space, whereas smaller spaces tend to produce more intense debate and polarised opinions (Sanoff, 2000). Discussions flow better when everyone can see each other, so a round table is ideal. The facilitator's position also influences dynamics; if they're positioned outside the group, participants are more likely to talk to each other.

The day will run more smoothly with one or two colleagues helping out: greeting people as they arrive, taking care of refreshments, setting up recording equipment and making notes. They will also be able to help review and analyse material afterwards. Recording the session is essential, whether audio or video, and the equipment must be tested before the session to ensure it will pick up everyone's voices clearly; a digital voice or audio recorder, or a video microphone with an omnidirectional setting works best with groups. Try and position recording equipment unobtrusively so participants are not conscious of it. Make sure batteries are fully charged and spares are on hand, that enough memory is available and that there's a back-up option just in case.

If it's possible to provide refreshments, then do so; participants will feel appreciated and more relaxed, and it helps create a more congenial atmosphere for discussion. For longer sessions it's almost always necessary, and can provide a welcome break. But don't have refreshments on the table during the session; eating and drinking sounds can easily obliterate the discussion!

Figure 7.2a

Figure 7.2b

Figure 7.2c

7.4	**RUNNING FOCUS GROUPS**

Everything about the session should be designed to put participants at ease, from the venue and room layout to a friendly welcome on the door and decent refreshments. This isn't just a matter of courtesy; relaxed participants yield good material. If people feel uncomfortable, they can become less forthcoming or more oppositional.

After introductions, the facilitator should briefly outline the event's purpose and time schedule, then check that everyone agrees to being recorded, ask if there are any questions, and set out confidentiality requirements and ground rules. Emphasise that the group is about sharing ideas, listening, debating and working constructively together: that everyone's contributions are equally valued, that there are no right or wrong answers, and that everyone should be treated courteously. Clarify that the facilitator's role is to guide the discussion and to listen, not to chair a meeting or lead the group. Keep preliminaries as brief as possible though; people have come to talk and will be keen to get started.

BIAS ISSUES IN
FOCUS GROUPS

PLANNING

Exclusion bias | Selection bias

Focus group participants are purposely chosen rather than self-selecting.
Consider whose voices will be heard and not heard, and what effect this will
have.

DATA COLLECTION

Interviewer bias | Procedural bias | Question-order bias

Consider whether the facilitator may have influenced the data by showing
positive or negative responses to views expressed, or spending more time
discussing favourable rather than unfavourable responses. Are there any
practical or logistical factors that could impact on the data, such as time,
venue, location or accessibility and assistance issues, which affect who can
participate? What effect will the structure of the event have on the data, in terms
of question order, covering topics, time allocation, etc?

ANALYSIS

Confirmation bias | Culture bias | Focusing effect | Group attribution error | Observer-expectancy effect | Stereotyping

Does analysis of the qualitative data offer new insights or only find what
was expected? Has all data been methodically analysed and considered or
have specific aspects become the main focus? Are participants viewed as
individuals expressing their personal opinions or as representatives of particular
demographic groups?

PARTICIPANTS

Acquiescence bias | Anchoring | Base rate fallacy | Bikeshedding | Concept test bias | Consistency bias | Dominant respondent bias | First speaker bias | Habituation bias | Halo effect | Hostility bias | Ingroup bias | Moderator acceptance bias | Overstatement bias | Reactive devaluation | Shared information bias | Sponsorship bias

A multitude of factors shape the group dynamic, participants' responses to the
substance of the discussion, and their level of engagement with the process –
all of which can create bias. A skilled facilitator can identify when these factors
come into play and manage them to some extent, but it's essential to consider
their effects in analysis.

See the Appendix for explanations of these types of bias.

Gathering data

The facilitator might start with an icebreaker exercise, depending on the group's make-up and purpose, or move straight on to the main business. As with the funnelling technique in questionnaires, start with factual and easily answered questions before discussing more complex issues.

Once the session is under way, the facilitator has two main tasks:

1. **Keeping to time.** This means balancing participants wanting to pursue issues of interest with the need to cover the topic schedule within the time available. A good knowledge of the matter under discussion will enable the facilitator to judge the potential value of conversational tangents.
2. **Ensuring that all participants contribute.** Any focus group will include talkative and reticent participants. The facilitator has to involve the reticent members, particularly in mixed groups, and manage the talkative ones. They might ask individuals to hold back so others can have their say, and the group may also self-regulate the discussion. To reduce the influence of more vociferous members and 'first speaker effect' (see the Appendix on types of bias) the facilitator can ask everyone to write down their responses to a question, then pool the answers for all to read.

One more thing that requires a facilitator's constant vigilance throughout a session is their own neutrality. The facilitator should mask their personal reactions to participants' views, guarding against verbal and non-verbal responses that imply approval or disapproval. As well as keeping comments and body language neutral, they need to give participants equal encouragement and time to speak, whether their comments are favourable or unfavourable, and avoid placing more emphasis on positive comments when summing up. This can be particularly challenging when designers run focus groups to get feedback on their work. But all participants' responses must be treated equally, and the facilitator should seek to build rapport, listening attentively to everyone and expressing interest through tone of voice and body language. If participants look to the facilitator for validation of their views, as often happens, they can deflect the question back to the group and ask what other people think. This is another argument in favour of the facilitator sitting a little outside the group, reducing the temptation for participants to look for their reactions. Another key aspect of neutrality is avoiding leading questions, which either imply a preferred answer or guide participants away from certain responses. Desired outcomes shouldn't shape how questions are worded.

The facilitator will need to take written notes during the session, without trying to capture every detail or being over-selective. It makes sense to record things beyond the substance of what was said: people's expressions, non-verbal responses, group dynamics, comments that caused a notable reaction, and so on. The facilitator can usefully spend a few minutes after participants have left reviewing their notes to check for clarity, adding in detail and explanation as required, highlighting any significant themes or connections, and noting anything unexpected that may need to be looked at further. They should hold off at this stage from forming interpretations, and focus on asking questions about the data rather than trying to find answers.

Activities and exercises

Activities and exercises in focus groups are completely optional. For some groups or topics, discussion alone will yield enough good material; other groups may be more responsive to interactive elements. As always, start with the desired end results, look at what information is required and then work backwards to find the best ways to obtain it. Given the time constraints, any activities should be quickly explainable, short, fun and/or interesting, and easy for participants to complete. (Lengthier and more complex tasks, or idea-generating exercises suit workshops better.) Activities that work in focus groups call for immediate personal responses without needing any prior knowledge, such as:

- **Prioritising/sorting exercises** using cards, post-it notes, etc.
- **Map- or model-based activities.** Ask participants to identify things like places that they like and dislike, or routes they prefer and those they avoid.
- **Image- or object-based activities.** Pictures or artefacts are a good way to generate discussion, and are also effective in working with more sensitive topics. 'Mood boards' and collage can help people consider design options and identify preferences.

A useful insight from UX focus group research is that if participants are shown images of a product concept, they can form an opinion, but if they're given a prototype to examine, they can give much more valuable feedback based on their first-hand experience. There's certainly scope to use focus groups to consider usability issues more in spatial design, using fly-throughs or physical and virtual models: something for designers to bear in mind.

During group activities, the facilitator should continue observing the proceedings, checking that everyone contributes. The process itself can be revealing and the insights it offers can be as useful as the outcome, so it can help to ask questions as participants work on their task to understand their thinking.

Close the session on a positive note with a simple or light-hearted question or two, especially if there were any difficult dynamics. Ask if anyone has any questions before the group breaks up, and outline what will happen to the material from the session, the next steps in the design and decision-making processes, and further opportunities for participation. Thank the group warmly for their time and input, and generally aim to make everyone feel glad they came. Send a follow-up email shortly afterwards thanking participants again, asking for feedback on the experience, and whether they would like updates on the project and future events Add them to the mailing list if so.

7.5	WORKING WITH FOCUS GROUP MATERIAL

Focus groups create a lot of material to consider. It's a good idea to produce a summary sheet for each session, detailing who was involved, the material collected, the relevant research objectives and questions, topics covered, and any comments on the session. Add this to the data library along with material produced by the group, video or audio transcripts, any photos and the facilitator's notes.

Download and back up video and audio recordings straight away. Reviewing and analysing these recordings can take time, which should be factored into the programme schedule. It will help if staff who attended can review a recording together and make an initial assessment of the material, which can start to guide the analysis. Before considering what participants actually said, begin by identifying the subjects that seemed most significant: those that kept cropping up throughout the session, that they discussed the most and that sparked intense discussion. Also notice silences, tensions, body language, looks and other non-verbal cues, which can provide useful information and contextualise participants' expressed views.

Managing data

There's no standard procedure for analysing the large amounts of complex qualitative material that focus groups produce, but the 'Quick guide to analysing qualitative data' gives some suggested steps. Often the first step is transcribing the discussion. This can take a lot of time (it's normal to spend an hour transcribing ten minutes of speech), so it may be necessary to select material to focus on, guided by the initial review. The time investment is worthwhile when a deeper analysis is needed, to discover the underlying reasons for people's attitudes or behaviour, for example (and if less depth is needed, focus groups are probably aren't the best method).

Analysing data

Qualitative data analysis always entails disassembling and reassembling material. This might involve investigating various themes, questions or types of users, but always using the same approach of taking data apart and rearranging it, and noting patterns and linkages that emerge. The disassembly stage involves pulling out everything relating to a subject, then tagging these data chunks with keywords and adding comments as necessary. Then start on the next subject, pull out all relevant chunks, add new keywords and comments, and repeat with all the remaining subjects.

A common approach to this phase in UX is affinity diagramming. This is an interactive visual method of identifying themes within the data, which starts by summarising each comment on a post-it note, and then clustering together comments relating to specific objectives or themes that emerge during analysis (see Figure 7.3). It works well for smaller datasets, short programmes or where there aren't a wide range of issues under consideration. For large and/or complex datasets, I recommend coding, employed widely in qualitative analysis in social science. This entails creating a structure of categories and keywords to index the data, and then filtering, sorting, and cross-referencing to identify themes and connections. The 'Quick guide to analysing qualitative data' gives more detail. Both approaches can be usefully done as a team, using index cards or post-it notes, maps and plans of the scheme, and the results of desk research and any previous engagement work, for context.

Whatever the method, the key tasks are to compare and contrast within the material, looking for similarities and differences, patterns and relationships, consistencies and inconsistencies, and the unexpected and anomalous. Designers and visual thinkers will probably find that sketching diagrams, flow charts, mind maps and so on help in exploring and giving coherence to the data. As visually presented information is more accessible and engaging for many laypeople too, these sketches are worth keeping for future communications. It's also important to keep questioning throughout this stage. Are we asking the right questions, and the right people? Does this data confirm or contradict findings from other research?

115

Drawing conclusions

If focus groups are held at the initial stages of a project to understand the general local context, it will be too early to draw conclusions, so it's best just to summarise the range of topics covered, the main areas of interest or concern, and suggestions for next steps. For focus groups dealing with more specific issues, the interpretation process should be guided by the research questions. It's important to bring all the relevant content into the interpretation phase, and to resist the temptation to cherry-pick the more interesting material or that which supports a desired outcome. Recalling the validity and reliability imperatives (see section 2.2), analyse data impartially and represent it truthfully. However, remember that focus groups aren't a microcosm of the wider community, and findings aren't generalisable; it's impossible to know whether participants' views are representative, or how much weight can be given to them. And studies have shown flaws in 'groupthink'; for example, people can find other group members' opinions more convincing than the factual information given (Weinschenk, 2011).

Figure 7.3
Affinity diagramming

7.6   KEY POINTS SUMMARY

> Focus groups give insight into people's opinions, feelings, preferences and experiences, with group dynamics playing an important role in shaping the debate.

The role of facilitator is key; it requires a high level of people skills, as well as an understanding of the local context and the proposal.

A focus group should have a clear aim, reflecting the research objectives with a carefully planned schedule of topics to cover.

Exercise selectivity in inviting participants – they have to be the right people to answer the questions.

Venue and room layout can affect how people respond and interact, and should be chosen with care.

Activities and exercises can complement group discussion and offer different perspectives that talking might not.

Working with the complex data generated by a focus group takes time and skill. It will often need to be transcribed, coded, disassembled and reassembled before any interpretation can begin.

Effective communication starts by putting yourself in another's position. If you understand where people are coming from, you'll be able to communicate more clearly, and build trust and rapport.

Respect local knowledge. Local people are the experts on their environment and can offer insight that you don't have, so ensure there is plenty of opportunity for them to do so.

Be open about the nature of the development and the options for the site. What in the proposal can and can't be changed, and what the options are, for example.

Get feedback on communications before going live, preferably from non-professionals. Check that information materials, web content, media copy and publicity is engaging and hits the right note.

Proactively reach out to marginalised groups to encourage their participation from the outset. Go and meet them on their own terms first to start a dialogue, and be prepared to work with groups with specific needs separately.

Utilise many communications channels. Maximising selected online platforms is essential, but local print media, posters and leaflets can reach larger numbers of people.

Take care not to present proposals in a way that implies that decisions have already been made when they haven't. Presenting detailed designs at an early stage of consultations says 'This is what we are going to do', rather than 'This is what we *could* do.' Begin a dialogue with the community and get their thoughts before starting any design work whenever possible.

Provide the information people need to make up their own minds about a development from the start, rather than trying to win them over (which can have the opposite effect).

Have visible information about the proposed development around the vicinity of the site, especially for public realm projects, which passers-by and regular users of the space will see.

Use more images and fewer words. Make sure they're images that are comprehensible to the non-professional, which meaningfully reflect the local area to the people who live there.

Aim for 'cognitive ease'. Communicate using concepts and illustrations that people are comfortable with. Refer to the familiar, well known and tangible. This helps build rapport and credibility.

All public communications should use clear everyday language that everyone can understand (aim for a reading age of 12). There is no need to dumb down – just avoid jargon, abbreviations, technical terminology, corporate buzzwords and design-speak.

Aim to get a wide range of feedback rather than as many responses as possible. Targeted communications may be needed to engage some groups.

Show empathy and be a good listener. Try to understand the potential effects of the proposed development on local people and listen to their concerns. Ensure they have opportunities to discuss those, even if they can't be resolved by the design team.

Ongoing communication is essential to build trust and enable continuing discussion. A report on the event, articles in the local press, a newsletter, a dedicated website, social media or a liaison group for bigger projects can facilitate this.

Get feedback on communications whenever possible. For example, 'What do you think of our website?' and 'How did you find completing this survey?' and act on the responses.

8 Collaborative approaches

8.1	INTRODUCTION

We've now reached 'Involve' and 'Collaborate' on the Spectrum of Participation, bringing local people and designers together to work on ideas at events such as charrettes, workshops, neighbourhood planning days and co-design programmes. These events involve similar approaches to preparation, communication and information gathering. This chapter therefore focuses on creating meaningful collaborative opportunities that generate good material and looks at the implications of working at this level for designers and for the community.

COLLABORATIVE
APPROACHES

Methodology type:
qualitative

Level of participation:
involve/collaborate

Time/resource needed for data collection:
medium | high

Time/resource needed for data analysis:
high

Useful for:
understanding site context
understanding attitudes/perceptions/values/feelings
testing/getting opinions/feedback
understanding behaviour/interactions/use of space
site planning/generating ideas
design development

8.2 **COLLABORATIVE APPROACHES**

Core values of participation

The International Association for Public Participation (IAP2.org) sets out seven core values that should underpin public participation in any context, which certainly apply to collaborative approaches on spatial design projects, and would usefully inform the planning of any programme.

Public participation:

1. Is based on the belief that those who are affected by a decision have a right to be involved in the decision-making process.
2. Includes the promise that the public's contribution will influence the decision.
3. Promotes sustainable decisions by recognising and communicating the needs and interests of all participants, including decision-makers.
4. Seeks out and facilitates the involvement of those potentially affected by or interested in a decision.
5. Seeks input from participants in designing participation processes.
6. Provides participants with the information they need to participate in a meaningful way.
7. Communicates to participants how their input affected the decision.

Types of events

Collaborative work is all about people-centred design. If participants can be involved in planning the collaboration process itself and helping to decide the forms of participation, even better. Some practices and clients will prefer to stick with tried and trusted methods, but collaborative approaches can and should use a range of different ways to involve people. There are ready-made toolkits such as Planning for Real, Crowd Wise, Enquiry by Design, Placecheck, Spaceshaper, and others, which offer templates and resources for local community participation events. There's also a multitude of options for activities: planning days, visioning events, design workshops, charrettes, mapping and modelling sessions, transect walks, local surveys, community profiling, art projects and co-design programmes, to name but a few. Nick Wates' indispensable *The Community planning handbook* (Wates, 2014) offers a wealth of ideas, and I strongly advise getting a copy or visiting the online version at communityplanning.net to explore the possibilities.

Working with groups

Creating enjoyable events is a serious matter; they're more likely to generate good information, and good information helps generate good design. Collaborative activities are open to all, and people get involved for all sorts of reasons, with differing levels of investment and (self-)interest. But what all participants bring is local knowledge. Skilful facilitation is key to making the most this essential resource; if the team on the day can focus on building group cohesion, enabling everyone to contribute fully, listening well, and offering something back to participants, they should be more inclined to contribute their local expertise.

Figure 8.1a

Figure 8.1b

Figure 8.1c

A good participation programme should result in people feeling that a project reflects their wishes and needs, inspiring a sense of ownership and local pride, and building social capital. Equally important is that participants work not only with designers but also with each other, making connections and creating lasting relationships, thereby also building 'emotional capital' (Ermacora and Bullivant, 2015). Participation programmes should endeavour to provide people with opportunities to develop their networks, and their investment in the local area and its communities. It may cost designers a little more time and energy but this can be an invaluable legacy, especially in deprived areas and those undergoing major changes.

Figure 8.2
Look for ways to build social and emotional capital

8.3   PREPARATION

Figure 8.3
Suggested workshop process

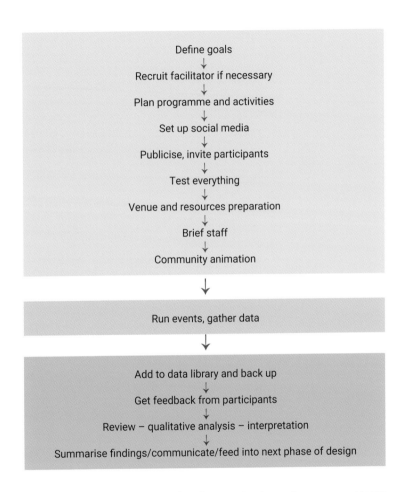

Collaborative processes require a lot of preparation, in event management terms and as a research activity; see Figure 8.3 for a suggested process. Before doing anything, decide good goals for the event which contribute in specific ways to the project's research questions and provide positive outcomes for participants. Be open about them so people know what's in it for them (and there *must* be something in it for them). The fact that public events are open to anyone makes it impossible to predict how they will go on the day, so build some flexibility into the programme. Perhaps have some alternative activities ready if those planned don't seem appropriate when the time comes – if there are too many attendees for them to work well, for instance – and make contingency plans for other elements of the programme that could go awry. In other words, expect the unexpected.

It should go without saying that a viable time schedule is essential. Don't try to cram too much in, and allow plenty of time for tasks and interaction. Are any activities being used for the first time? Pilot them, to check that everything works as needed and to allocate enough time. The team should run through the schedule and responsibilities together before an event in any case, and remind themselves of the purpose of the exercise in the context of the overall research plan.

Gathering data

Staff responsible for video recording, photography and note-taking have particularly important roles. They need to prepare thoroughly in terms of checking equipment and logistics, and on the day they need to observe as well as record interactions and group dynamics. It's important to note participants' decision-making processes or trains of thought in group activities, not just the outcomes of their deliberations. So ask questions while groups are working and find out what's behind their choices. Observations on their priorities, criteria for decisions or alternatives they rejected can inform the ensuing design work as much as the plans they did produce. Err on the side of collecting too much material rather than too little. Without disrupting the proceedings, take plenty of photos, record lots of video, talk to participants, make notes and sketches, and generally record as much activity as possible, however insignificant it may seem at the time.

Community animation

The better the design team's understanding of the local area and its communities, the more successful events are likely to be. This entails taking time to explore the area, talking to people in the street, generating interest and looking for ways to design events that will be relevant to the locality and local demographics: also known as community animation. It's possible to adopt a one-size-fits-all approach and run the same event format in different localities, but if a diverse range of participants is sought – and it should be – this won't always be the most effective way to engage them.

Practitioners working with local communities often encounter an endemic belief that there's no point in getting involved in participation programmes. Many people believe – not without reason – that they have no voice, no influence and that no one wants to listen to them. Designers and clients shouldn't underestimate the depth of this sense of powerlessness and exclusion, particularly in poorer areas and amongst marginalised groups. So how can designers respond to these feelings? They can initiate conversations from the outset, and listen, to try and understand the potential barriers. If practices look to build relationships, rather than merely harvest views, they'll be better able to address cynicism towards the process as well as concerns about the development itself.

Publicity

Once the objectives are settled, the event planned, resources prepared, staff roles allocated and the community animated, it's time to start on publicity. Collaborative approaches require a lot of time and energy from participants, but what's in it for them? An event needs to be presented as something meaningful to the community with an immediate appeal. Stock phrases like 'We want to hear from you', or 'Have your say' aren't always enough to persuade people to give up their leisure hours to attend an event, so be specific about what they can gain: learning new skills, meeting people, improving the neighbourhood, sharing ideas and knowledge and being part of creating something worthwhile, for a start. Attractive communications can be the deciding factor in capturing local interest. It's possible to use the same house-style template for all events but, again, it may not draw in a diverse range of participants. A unique 'brand' identity referencing the location is a better approach, with a positive look and feel designed for a wide appeal in that area. Designing the brand can also help the team synthesise their desk research and observation, and focus on the locality's defining characteristics.

Longer-term participation programmes and those relating to more complex sites or large populations need to use social media, and use it well. Social media functionality is evolving too rapidly to discuss here without the risk of immediate obsolescence, but there are some eternal verities to note, regardless of platform or audience:

- Social media channels should have specific individuals responsible for updates and development.
- Be selective about channels; only start using a new one if it's certain to be maintained.
- Post the same key messages and announcements across all platforms.
- Always give a response to queries and comments, and quickly.

129

- Expect people who are opposed to the development or unhappy with the process to take to social media to air their grievances; respond with courtesy, professionalism and openness.
- Avoid prolonged public arguments – but don't dodge questions.

BIAS ISSUES IN COLLABORATIVE APPROACHES	**PLANNING**
	**Exclusion bias	Selection bias**
	Whose voices are being heard and are not being heard? What effect will this have on the data?
	DATA COLLECTION
	**Procedural bias	Question-order bias**
	Are there any practical or logistical factors that could impact on the data, such as time, venue, location or accessibility and assistance issues, which affect who can participate? How will the structure of the event affect the data, particularly the order in which topics are covered, time allocation, etc?
	ANALYSIS
	**Confirmation bias	Culture bias	Focusing effect	Group attribution error	Observer-expectancy effect	Stereotyping**
	Is analysis of the qualitative data offering new insights or only finding what was expected? Has all data been methodically analysed and considered or have some specific aspects become the main focus? Are participants viewed as individuals expressing their personal opinions, or as representatives of particular demographic groups?
	PARTICIPANTS
	**Acquiescence bias	Anchoring	Base rate fallacy	Bikeshedding	Dominant respondent bias	Framing effect	Hostility bias	Ingroup bias	Moderator acceptance bias	Overstatement bias	Reactive devaluation	Shared information bias**
	A multitude of factors shape the group dynamic, how people respond to the substance of the discussion, and their level of engagement with the process – all of which can bias the data. A skilled facilitator can identify when these factors come into play and manage them to some extent but it's essential their effects are considered during the analysis process.
	See the Appendix for explanations of these types of bias.

A skilfully facilitated group becomes more than the sum of its parts in generating ideas: the hive-mind in action. It's important to establish a sense of common ground to get disparate individuals working as an effective group. Even if there are very different views within the group on issues or desired outcomes, a shared concern for the local environment is a strong uniting factor for the facilitator to build on, encouraging everyone to work together with a feeling of collective purpose. Involving the group in setting the agenda and deciding the programme structure also improves cohesion. A group that feels ownership of the process from the start is likely to work with a greater sense of responsibility for its tasks, and will generate more authentic and carefully considered ideas.

Communication

In a collaborative process, designers and local people sit down together to work. This means staff facilitating design activities, answering questions and enabling people to make informed decisions, as well as gathering material. This close level of interaction requires staff to be aware of how they present themselves, without becoming painfully self-conscious – to choose their words carefully, staying neutral, professional and clear. It's my perception that listening skills make all the difference to being accepted as an honest broker by participants and communities. When designers appear not to be listening, participation programmes become seen as tick-box exercises. This means listening both at a personal interaction level and as a practice in its relationship with a community.

Experienced practitioners say that honesty from the start is also essential, so be open about the range of possible outcomes and the influence that the public can have on the proposal. And be clear about which aspects are negotiable, as well as budget, planning constraints, the client's requirements and other parameters. (Interviewees in Chapter 10 refer to believing that collaborative processes would have given them more say in the final design than was the case, for instance.)

Designers take on a moral obligation to communities when they invite them to collaborate as partners on a project. Local hopes and aspirations are stirred and expectations are raised. Whatever the scope of the project, the designer's role is to work with local people to get the best outcomes for them. Each community is different and has different priorities, so listening and learning about those priorities from the start is the key to gaining trust and building good relationships. The final plans generated by collaborative approaches should reflect the aspirations and needs communicated during the programme as far as possible. This means working the material into the design impartially and honestly (and offering an honest explanation if popular ideas were rejected).

Figure 8.4
A guided walk

Giving to participants

I've already mentioned that participants should receive something worthwhile in exchange for the considerable time and energy they'll devote to collaborative events. Longer-term processes can provide participants with valuable learning opportunities, offering not only personal development but also enabling their more meaningful ongoing contribution, and building community capacity and confidence. However keen people are to get involved, a principle of reciprocity is vital, and even more so when enthusiasm is less abundant. What then can participants take away with them?

Skills and knowledge. Collaborative programmes can give an insight into design processes and how designers work, a world shrouded in mystery for many. Participants will often be interested in trying out the software tools that designers work with and learning some basics; this is an especially worthwhile offer for young people or marginalised groups. Are there opportunities to share knowledge or teach other skills, design-related or otherwise? Then make the most of them. All participants should leave having learned something new. For instance, this could be an introduction to aspects of design work, architecture, landscape or local history, or visiting other sites or projects. Charrettes involving specialists in a range of areas are particularly ripe for providing learning opportunities and sharing expertise.

Fun and stimulation. Fun activities have a deceptively important function. They build cohesion and identity, help participants get to know each other, give a chance to relax mentally and a break from thinking about difficult issues, bring some physical exertion into what can otherwise be very sedentary work, and allow laughter and a release for any tension. Games and quizzes can break up the day by doing something just for fun, whereas activities with maps and models, or creating collages or artwork, for instance, can provide also useful material.

New relationships. Community participation programmes bring people together with a shared purpose, if not necessarily shared views, and can be a fertile environment for growing new connections and networks. Giving participants space to find common ground with each other and develop relationships is a valuable opportunity that designers can and should offer. It builds a greater sense of belonging to, and an awareness of, the local area and its issues, which can only benefit the process in hand, as well as building social capital for further community-driven initiatives.

Improving the site. Include some activity around the site if possible. This could be a community clean-up, planting, decorating, art projects, photography, video or performances featuring the site in some way. These help generate a sense of commitment and ownership, and can also raise awareness of the participation programme and the proposals.

A good event will first and foremost be engaging, relevant and appropriate to the intended participants. A mix of approaches that includes some sit-down group work, some outdoor activities, some cohesion-building time, some fun, some learning and some socialising should offer something for everyone – and provide a good range of material. As public events are open to all, aim to design activities everyone can join in equally and won't exclude anyone with, say, reduced mobility, sensory impairments, English as a second language or low literacy. Keep in touch with participants afterwards, if possible, and get their feedback. Encourage everyone to sign up for email updates; most will want to see any reports on the outcome of the events in which they participated, and hear about the project's progress.

8.5	WORKING WITH THE DATA

Collaborative methods produce qualitative data in considerable amounts. However, whatever the quantity, type of event, number of participants or projected outcome, the advice on working with data remains the same: review, sort, categorise, code, cluster, analyse, repeat.

Nonetheless, this can be a daunting prospect when there's a large amount of material. Unfortunately, there are no shortcuts; the good news, however, is that an intelligent strategy, clear research objectives from the outset, and a methodical approach to categorising and coding material will make this a more straightforward task than it may appear.

After each event, transcribe relevant excerpts of any video or audio recording, and add these to the data library along with material produced by the participants, any photos, facilitator's and staff notes, all of which should be backed up first, of course. Arrange for the team that was present on the day to review the event and make an initial assessment of the material; this can help guide the analysis and offer some useful insights. Then start work on the analysis proper as soon as possible, to identify points to work into the ongoing design process.

Preparing and analysing data

The 'Quick guide to analysing qualitative data' on p. 60 suggests structures for sorting, categorising and coding qualitative material for analysis. Qualitative material is always likely to be more complex and offer multiple interpretations, so have more than one person analysing the material if possible to reduce bias, as well as to share the workload. An advantage in analysing large datasets is that significant patterns and trends can be easier to spot, and data is more likely to fall into obvious clusters. Data that doesn't fit into emerging clusters shouldn't be disregarded though. Even if a strong majority view is clear, for instance, differing views ought still to receive the same level of analytical attention, and a large dataset will probably contain a greater range of views to consider. The principle remains that the analysis includes the full range of views; check the 'Quick guide to reporting research' on p. 136 for more advice.

8.6   KEY POINTS SUMMARY

> Collaborative processes give participants decision-making power in the design of the process and more influence generally than other approaches. There's also greater emphasis on working together and learning.

Creative participation processes require more preparation than more standardised approaches, and for flexibility and contingency plans to be included in the programme.

Think about creating ways to allow people to offer the most useful information they can.

Collaborative programmes demand an especially good understanding of the local area and its communities, so they're appealing and relevant to as wide a range of people as possible.

People often need to be persuaded that there's a point in getting involved, and to be convinced that their voices will be heard.

Social media is essential but requires careful handling if it's to be an asset rather than a liability.

Professionals should treat local people as colleagues and partners collaborating on a project, and actively work to foster trust, develop communications and build good relationships.

Make sure participants leave having gained something: for example, skills, knowledge, new contacts, new interests or a sense of having done something worthwhile to improve the local area.

The material gathered will take a lot of working through, so allow enough staff time for this.

A good report has a clear structure and narrative. It's free of jargon, waffle and errors, and has been copy-edited and proofread. Add data or materials from events as appendices, and an executive summary setting out the issues, methods, key findings and recommendations.

Structure the report by topic, theme or research objectives, using qualitative and quantitative material in the narrative.

To ensure validity (see section 2.2), consider all the data, and draw findings and conclusions directly from the data.

Be impartial. Avoid giving undue prominence to particular views, especially those that are more positive towards the proposal.

Report on the whole range of views expressed, not just the majority, and include odd and inconsistent findings; it can all provide useful insight.

Show how recommendations or options were derived from the data, to allow readers to decide whether they're correct.

Include a section explaining the research methods, including how participants were recruited, and whether any groups are over- or under-represented, for transparency.

Get feedback from participants on a draft of the full report before publication if possible. Participants should always be able to see full reports on the research.

Consider producing findings in different formats for different audiences. For example, videos or animations may sometimes be more accessible than text-based reports.

Disseminate widely. What could other practitioners or clients learn from the project? Publish articles and blog posts to share your knowledge.

REPORTING STATISTICS

Include some supporting information to help contextualise statistics from surveys:
- **Response rate:** responses received as a percentage of the total possible number of responses, if known. If 1,000 questionnaires are sent out and 200 returned, the response rate is 20%.
- **Frequency:** the total number of responses to a question or in a category.

- **Mean:** the average when numerical values (for example, scores or ratings) are added together and divided by the number of responses.
- **Median:** the numerical value midway between the highest and lowest values.
- **Mode:** the most common response overall.

Mean, median and mode averages would identify the most popular choices if participants were asked to rank some options or select their top three preferences from a list, for example.

Explain what the data shows, rather than just present the raw figures.

Responses from some groups may vary from the aggregate. Highlight these so that the majority view isn't assumed to represent all groups. But remember that comparisons aren't reliable within small samples or with a low response rate.

Ethical practice is vital in the reporting stage in giving an honest and transparent account of findings. It's unethical to:

- **adjust** data to support a particular narrative or outcome
- **exclude** data that doesn't support a particular narrative or outcome
- **falsify** data by manipulation or fabrication
- **overstate** the significance of findings
- **misrepresent** participants' views.

VISUALISING INFORMATION

Use widely understood formats to represent quantitative data, such as:
- **Pie charts** to show the percentages of a whole where these add up to 100%, for example the share of votes for each choice in a ballot.
- **Bar charts** to show actual numbers of cases, for example the numbers of votes for each option.
- **Line charts** to show the relationship between two or more variables, for example how male and female voters responded to each option, highlighting differences and similarities.

Qualitative data needs descriptive text but can be complemented with infographics, flowcharts and timelines to present narratives and processes, and word-clouds and mind maps to show conceptual frameworks.

Keep it simple; don't put too much information in one graphic, and ensure text is legible.

Choose contrasting colours for graphics, as not everyone can discern subtle differences.

Desire Lines: A Guide to Community Participation in Designing Places

9 Ethical and inclusive practice

9.1	INTRODUCTION

The four key research principles introduced in Chapter 2 underpin the advice offered throughout this book, namely:

- reliability
- validity
- impartiality
- ethical practice.

Ethical practice merits further discussion in its own right, however, as it should inform and shape all aspects of a participation programme. To restate a point made earlier, ethics shouldn't be thought of as rules about what not to do, but pointers to how to do things better. This chapter starts by looking at ethical practice at each stage of the research process, from project planning to working with participants, to analysis and reporting. It then covers inclusive design with (not for) people with disabilities and marginalised groups, and offers guidance on working with children and young people, with particular regard to informed consent and safeguarding requirements.

9.2	RESEARCH ETHICS

What are research ethics?

There are three broad categories of ethical requirements that guide research in any field where human behaviour is the subject of study. These cover:

1. Safeguarding participants, and those conducting the research.
2. Treating participants with respect.
3. Maintaining high standards of integrity and professionalism in conducting research.

So how are these ethical principles relevant to designers working with communities?

The first category, **safeguarding participants and those conducting the research**, means taking responsibility for a duty of care for people attending events and participating in activities, and for staff involved. This refers to ensuring physical safety and avoiding emotional distress, and might typically include:

- **Assessing potential risks** to participants and staff engaged on the project, and taking necessary measures to protect their health and safety.
- **Informed consent.** Provide all the information people need to decide whether to participate at the outset, including what will be involved, times, venue and any risks or benefits.
- **Not doing harm**. No research should involve any physical or emotional suffering for participants, or any potential loss of privacy, dignity or reputation.
- Staff being competent to **respond appropriately to sensitive topics or difficult situations** that arise. For example, discussions about local crime or antisocial behaviour could bring up feelings of anxiety and fear for some, or be a reminder of distressing experiences. Emotive topics, or those where opinion is sharply divided, can become heated and staff need to know when and how to intervene.

The second set of ethical requirements relates to **treating participants with respect**. This is about recognising their rights, creating optimum conditions for them to contribute to the programme and designing out barriers (discussed in more detail in section 9.3). They cover aspects such as:

- Looking at the event from the point of view of a range of different prospective participants to identify any **obstacles or deterrents to participation**, whether physical, logistical, cultural or cognitive.
- Giving particular consideration to measures to **maximise the participation** of people with additional needs and marginalised groups – not just removing barriers but actively seeking their participation.
- **Designing and conducting programmes** that acknowledge participants' concerns, values, needs, expertise and dignity, which involve activities in which all are fully able to participate.
- **Staff being courteous, approachable and professional** at all times.
- **Voluntary participation:** assure participants that they're under no obligation to get involved, and have the right to withdraw at any time and for any reason.
- **Checking the findings and analysis with participants** if possible, and keeping them informed of the research outcomes.
- **Making sure participants benefit** in some way from their involvement.

The final set of ethical requirements refers to **maintaining high standards of integrity and professionalism in conducting research**, including good governance within the practice, so that for example:

- **Lines of responsibility and accountability** within the design-research team are clearly defined.
- **Data is stored securely**, treated confidentially and is accessible only to those who need it.
- **Employers offer guidance and support** to those conducting research, especially when it may involve challenging issues or situations.
- **Staff are encouraged to reflect on and discuss the participation process**, and ethical issues in particular. This makes the project a learning opportunity for staff, and develops their insight and skills.
- **Research projects are conducted impartially** and free from personal, organisational and political bias. This can be a grey area when a practice designing a project is also consulting on it and the client is keen to see it implemented in line with their wishes. But the principle stands that the research strategy should be as bias-free as possible (refer to the Appendix for sources of bias), and aim to obtain reliable, valid data that supports evidence-based decision-making, with as much meaningful community input as circumstances permit.

Ethical project planning

Building ethical practice into a research project starts at the outset by creating a process that's inclusive, representative, transparent and as impartial as it can be. If possible, bring local people into designing the programme and advising on approaches that are likely to succeed. Make use of local knowledge and experience, and talk with groups who have already been involved in previous programmes (yours won't be the first, remember) to find out what works and what doesn't before deciding how to proceed; this saves time and energy for everyone. The more involvement people have from the start, the greater the likelihood that trust, goodwill and positive working relationships will follow.

Inclusivity involves proactively engaging with those who might not otherwise participate, whether due to physical, cultural or language barriers. Even with less participative methods like exhibitions and meetings, personally invite groups who are less likely to attend. Better still, take the exhibition or meeting to them. Also remember that any development can be an emotive issue for people. They can feel anxious or angry about proposed changes to their local environment, even more so if they believe they aren't being fully informed. Good communication and transparency can help allay these concerns. Present the facts clearly from the outset and aim to inform rather than persuade.

Ethical data gathering

To recap some ethical aspects of the data collection methods covered in previous chapters:

- **Observation.** Photography and video recording in a public space require discretion and sensitivity. Respect personal privacy, and don't record people in difficulties or engaged in illicit acts.
- **Photo and video diaries.** Participants should be asked not to photograph or video friends or family members for confidentiality reasons, and should be advised about personal safety and respecting others' privacy.
- **Focus groups.** Participants should agree to the group's confidentiality and privacy requirements, and any ground rules that need to be spelled out regarding respectful communication and behaviour. Staff have an ethical responsibility to report on events objectively, presenting as faithful an account as possible of the proceedings.
- **Meetings, exhibitions and collaborative processes.** Larger scale and more impersonal public events perhaps have fewer ethical factors to consider; the imperative is to make the event welcoming and inclusive to all, and to make sure everyone has an equal chance to put their views across. Again, staff should report the proceedings objectively and present an impartial analysis that acknowledges any possible bias.

Informed consent is important in diary studies and focus groups. Participants must be clear about the purpose of the research and any potential risks or benefits to them. They should freely agree to participate and understand that they can withdraw any time for any reason. They should also be clear about confidentiality rules and any publication or reporting of the research. These are standard informed consent conditions for any formal research involving human subjects, and while they may sound a little draconian in a design context, they're a useful reminder of the rights and responsibilities on both sides.

Finally, get participants' feedback on the process at every step of data gathering for evaluation. This benefits the project and gives the programme credibility, as well as demonstrating an ethical, collaborative approach to stakeholders such as the client, local authority or funders.

Ethical analysis and reporting

After data has been collected, ethical practice continues to inform the process of analysing and communicating the findings. Muratovski (2016) lists four cardinal sins for designers to avoid in this phase of work:

1. **Data fabrication:** adjusting data or filling gaps to support a desired outcome.
2. **Data elimination:** excluding data that's atypical or contrary to the prevalent view. Consider and report the full range of opinions or behaviour, not just the majority.
3. **Data exploitation:** making undue claims for findings or overstating their significance.
4. **Plagiarism:** representing another's work or data as your own. Always give credit where it's due.

This advice echoes the UK Research Integrity Office's policy on research conduct (2009), a standard widely adopted in many research areas. This policy additionally includes:

- **Falsification of data**, by the manipulation and/or selection of data, imagery, or consents.
- **Misrepresentation** by not reporting relevant findings and/or data accurately, or presenting a flawed interpretation of data, knowingly or otherwise (see 'How to lie (unintentionally) with statistics', below, for examples).
- **Failure to exercise due care** by allowing unreasonable risk or harm to people, or mismanaging privileged or private information collected during the research.

HOW TO LIE
(UNINTENTIONALLY)
WITH STATISTICS

These are two examples from a real project showing the need to handle statistics with care.

A local authority ran a series of consultation events on the regeneration of a large housing estate and recorded the attendance numbers:

Site visits (2): 38
Workshops (4): 86
Exhibitions (3): 193
Meetings (2): 268
Total number of people attending: 452

What's wrong with this? Some people might have attended several events. Some might have attended every single one. So the 'Total number of people attending' figure is almost certainly overstated.

The same authority also ran a public exhibition on the estate with a feedback form on the proposals for residents to complete. Of the estate's 6,000+ residents, 133 attended and 100 left comments, of which 82 were positive. The report stated that '82% of residents completing a feedback form were in favour of the scheme', concluding that this indicated residents' 'clear support' for the proposals. Were the views of this small percentage of residents representative of the whole estate? Statistically, it's pretty unlikely. (The 'Quick guide to reporting research' on p. 136 has tips on how to contextualise statistics and avoid this kind of misrepresentation.)

9.3	**INCLUSIVE PRACTICE**

Some groups can be unwittingly excluded or discouraged from participating in engagement processes. This section looks at the barriers that can deter or prevent those who are less likely to be heard from contributing to participation programmes, and how designers can actively address these. For the sake of broad categorisation, I've characterised these as physical/cognitive barriers and social/cultural barriers. I focus in this section on the obstacles rather than the groups who experience them. For example, wheelchair users aren't the problem: poor accessibility is.

Physical and cognitive barriers

There are around 13 million people with disabilities in the UK, or almost 1 in 5 of the population (Department for Work and Pensions, 2017). Under the Equality Act 2010, this means anyone reporting a long-standing illness, disability or impairment that causes substantial difficulty with day-to-day activities. This includes a vast array of conditions and needs, some visible and many not. It's essential to engage with people with a range of disabilities to discuss relevant issues in the proposal. Designers need to design *with* people with disabilities not *for* them, and excellent design can only come about when these groups are involved. A sighted or hearing designer cannot know what it's like to be visually or hearing impaired, for instance. They can gain useful awareness from temporarily experiencing being unable to see or hear and trying to navigate the streets, but it's a world of difference from living with permanent sensory impairment and enduring the everyday frustrations created by poor design. Physical obstructions can also present insurmountable barriers, such that people with disabilities are 'designed out' completely.

Diary studies or photo or video journals can provide invaluable insight into these issues, showing designers how they can make environments usable and welcoming, and avoid including needlessly disabling features. There's also a strong argument for designers to spend time accompanying people with physical, sensory or cognitive impairments on their day-to-day local activities, such as shopping, using public transport and generally negotiating public space, to appreciate the obstacle courses they routinely encounter, and the strategies and information they bring to navigating this unnecessarily difficult terrain.

Furthermore, designers tend to focus on visual quality, but as Whyte's studies show, people aren't drawn to a space by aesthetics alone (Whyte, 1980). Other sensory factors, such as tactile, acoustic and olfactory qualities are also important, particularly to visually impaired users. Above all, people want comfort, shelter, a choice of sun or shade, good seating options and spaces where they can be sociable or solitary.

Spatial design that works for people with disabilities and impairments works for everyone, and the same applies to public events. This means ensuring venues are fully accessible, putting in helpful signage, and asking people if they'd like assistance rather than making assumptions or unsolicited interventions. In terms of information, keep words to a minimum and let self-explanatory images do the talking as much as possible. By exercising some empathy and common sense, it should be possible to make participation programmes accessible and relevant to all, with and without disabilities, with a resulting positive effect on design outcomes.

Figure 9.1
Good public space offers more than visual quality

Social and cultural barriers

Rapidly changing cities need new thinking about social space. Recent profound economic and demographic shifts have major consequences for many aspects of urban infrastructure and public space: a rapidly growing older population, increased longevity, more single-person and small households, high levels of transience in urban areas, less secure employment and housing ... the list goes on. Add to the mix loss of funding for local amenities like parks, libraries and children's play facilities, while public space is privatised by stealth, and spaces that were once open to all are now 'for customer use only'. Not forgetting gentrification, which can further erode local space as run-down areas are transformed into upmarket destinations, with established communities often the losers. In this context of irreversible major change, it's arguable that placemaking for inclusive, accessible and free public space has never been so important in urban life.

By focusing on placemaking that works for existing communities as well as for those who developers hope to draw in, it's feasible for regeneration to create successful, inclusive new spaces and amenities. Areas that are seen as ripe for development tend, of course, to be inhabited by greater concentrations of marginalised and impoverished communities, and this has to be factored into designing a meaningful participation programme. As I've already stressed, this means proactively contacting specific groups to invite them to contribute, and if possible working out a programme with them to increase engagement. Refer back to the High Line example on p. 9 for a reminder of why this matters.

A huge range of issues come under the heading of social and cultural barriers, so start by thinking about how different groups might respond to aspects of the programme. Try and see things from their perspective, identify deterrents that can be removed, consider how extra support and encouragement can be given to those who might welcome it, and aim to make events as relevant and engaging as possible for everyone.

9.4	WORKING WITH CHILDREN AND YOUNG PEOPLE

There are two main reasons for including a section on working with children and young people. Firstly, there are child-specific issues to address, and areas where practitioners must tread carefully. Secondly, it's vital to include children and young people's views, and to understand their needs, which requires skill and empathy. In working on projects such as town centres, estate regeneration, streets and parks, it's essential that all ages get the chance to participate, and children and young people bring very particular perspectives and a keen awareness of their local environment. Children's participation in decision-making and design should be a meaningful experience with positive rewards for them, and can give designers insights that they might not have otherwise had.

The advice in this section is based on the Market Research Society's Guidelines for Research with Children and Young People (2012). The MRS guidance is recognised as robust and relevant in social research and other research fields, and is based on a strong ethical foundation designed both to treat participants with respect and to improve the quality of research (note that these tend to go hand in hand). Although the guidance may not always translate readily into the world of the built environment professional, the ethical philosophy certainly does, and it may also provide fresh ideas for working with this age group. The MRS guidelines define children as under 16 and young people as 16–17 year-olds, which I'll also use here. It doesn't recommend a lower age limit for working with children, but suggests involving very young children only if necessary and appropriate.

Permission and consent

The guidance makes a vital distinction between 'permission' and 'consent' as they pertain to children's participation in a project, and sets out a two-stage process to obtain these:

1. **Parent's permission**. The researcher asks a parent or responsible adult's permission to invite the child to take part.
2. **Child's consent.** If the adult agrees, the researcher can then approach the child, giving them all the information they need to give their informed consent. The child may agree or decline to participate, as they freely choose.

The text box below suggests some basic information that could be needed for informed consent to be given. The guidance emphasises that although a responsible adult may give permission for a child to participate in a research project, the child isn't obliged to take part. While a formal process of seeking adults' permission and children's informed consent may not be practicable or necessary for every project involving working with children in a design context, the spirit of the guidance still stands, if not the letter. Adults and children need to know what the project involves, any potential risks, costs or other consequences, and children should be free whenever possible to decide whether they want to take part. It's a fundamental research principle that participants have the right to withdraw from a project at any stage, and this right extends equally to children and young people. If a project involving children is being conducted in partnership with a local school, as is often the case, it's recommended that if a teacher or other staff member acting *in loco parentis* gives their agreement, permission should still also be sought from parents or guardians.

INFORMED CONSENT	What do parents/carers and participants need in order to give permission and informed consent? As a minimum:

- Details of the client, the practice and a named contact on the project for further information.
- The purpose of the overall project and of this event or activity within it.
- What it will involve.
- Whether proceedings will be recorded and/or observed by whom, and who is likely to have access to recordings.
- Who will be supervising and who else will be present.
- The amount of time involved and overall time schedule.
- Any possible costs, risks or hazards involved.
- Uses to which photos or recordings may be put afterwards. (Obtain permission separately to reproduce images or video footage of children; some parents/carers may be happy for a photo to appear in the local paper but not in marketing material, for example.)

Data collection

Collecting data from children and young people differs from collecting data from adults. Whatever the method, whether using photo or video diaries, group discussions, design workshops, events, classroom-based or outdoor activities, there are some specific issues to bear in mind.

Information-gathering questions and activities should be age-appropriate; in other words, don't ask children about things they may not know about or understand, and keep language simple and clear. Use the methods best suited to gathering the required information. If statistics about children's opinions, preferences or regular activities are needed, then questionnaires, quizzes, polls and voting exercises are good ways to gather this. Insights into feelings, experiences and beliefs require qualitative approaches, such as group discussion, observation, games and creative activities. Most projects, as with adult participants, will benefit from a mixture of qualitative and quantitative methods. If possible, give participants the opportunity to contribute in a range of ways; some children will express themselves more easily through drawing or making things, whereas others will enjoy writing and quizzes more.

Participants of any age should never be steered towards giving certain responses, and this is particularly important when working with children and young people who are less likely to spot leading questions. There should be no suggestion that questions have right or preferred answers. While carved in tablets of stone for social researchers, realistically this is a less clear-cut matter in the built environment. Designers can be required to consult on and generate support for a scheme at the same time if the client's keen to persuade the local community of the proposal's merits. Nonetheless, ethical practice requires that whatever the client's desired outcomes, participants receive correct, complete and impartial information about the development, and the views they contribute are treated equally, whether positive or negative. This applies to children and young people as much as adults.

Child protection and safeguarding issues

The agencies to contact at the time of writing regarding working with children and vulnerable groups were the Disclosure and Barring Service (DBS) in England and Wales, Disclosure Scotland and AccessNI in Northern Ireland. Beyond the legal safeguarding requirements, there are some precautions to consider in ensuring children's safety and wellbeing as participants.

In terms of general safety, check for possible hazards first if events and activities are taking place outdoors or in premises with which the children aren't familiar. This is common sense up to a point, but look at the environment from a child's point of view and ensure it's safe, accessible and suitably equipped for the group concerned. Provide parents/carers with full details of the event's location and finish time if it's not school-based, and a phone number if they need to contact a member of staff.

If refreshments are on offer, the MRS guidelines recommend avoiding anything that can cause allergic problems, sweets and snacks that are high in fat, salt or sugar. Only have physical contact with children and young people if it's immediately needed to prevent harm or avert danger, or if they might require assistance, in which case ask first. Remembering the 'do no harm' requirement, think carefully about questions and activities that could cause young participants distress or anxiety. For instance, talking with children about problematic aspects of their local environment can bring up unpleasant experiences or fears, which will require sensitive handling. Finally, anonymise material before adding it to the data library, along with any family members' or friends' identifying details. If demographic information is required (and it shouldn't be collected unless it is needed), it's best if parents/carers give this at the permission and consent stage rather than asking participants. None of these concerns should deter designers at all from working with children and young people. They have so much to contribute, and participation provides great opportunities to excite children and young people about their environment and about design, so make the most of what they can offer and what you can offer them.

Figure 9.2

9.5   KEY POINTS SUMMARY

Ethical practice starts at a project's inception and permeates the research design, data collection, analysis and communication stages.

There are three main elements to ethical practice:
1. Safeguarding participants and those conducting the research.
2. Treating participants with respect.
3. Maintaining high standards of integrity and professionalism.

Specific attention should be paid to ways in which participation processes could exclude or deter some groups, whether by physical obstacles or cultural barriers. Building relationships with marginalised groups is vital, and either encouraging them to participate or taking the process to them to get their contributions.

Working with children and young people needs to be handled with special care. Permission to invite them should be sought from parents/carers, with the decision as to whether to participate given by children themselves.

Safeguarding responsibilities in working with children and young people must be considered.

Desire Lines: A Guide to Community Participation in Designing Places

10 Participants' experiences

10.1	INTRODUCTION

This final chapter gives participants the last word. I interviewed representatives from a range of local groups around the country to discuss their experiences of participation programmes, which include standard consultation exercises, lengthy co-design programmes, neighbourhood planning processes and small-scale collaborative projects. Excerpts from those discussions are grouped roughly under common themes, and are intended as anecdotal illustration of the range of experiences rather than a representative cross-section. Participants are quoted verbatim as far as possible, and are intentionally anonymised.

10.2	MOTIVATIONS

Why do people devote significant amounts of time and energy to engagement programmes? They want to hold developers to account and ensure that developments benefit local people without damaging local businesses or valued aspects of the local character. All the individuals and groups I spoke to were noticeably motivated by a sense of 'the greater good' rather than their own personal interests.

'Most residents aren't nimbys, objecting to everything. They just want appropriate development to go ahead. We need housing, but let's not destroy all the unique reasons why people are attracted to living here in the first place.'

'We don't claim to be experts in planning but we want to see that things are done properly. We check whether the developer is presenting a clear picture of what they're doing, because it's important to have clarity about new developments and their potential impacts, but that's not always the case. Most developers will give as much information as they're required to but no more, and they won't highlight aspects that are problematic if they don't have to.'

'We focus mainly on conservation and preserving the historic character of the town, but without stifling economic activity. Places change and continue to change, and we have to keep the best parts but move with the times. We're not trying to preserve the town in aspic.'

COMMUNICATIONS AND COLLABORATION

The comments in this section suggest that while local groups are willing and able to collaborate, there's often a reticence on the part of designers and developers to bring them more fully into the process – or sometimes not invite them at all. The groups I spoke to all had an impressive range of valuable knowledge within their memberships, from professional planning and design expertise to local politics and community mobilisation. There was a sense of frustration, however, at the lack of opportunities to offer these skills and expert knowledge of local issues. There was also a strong feeling that more could be done to publicise engagement programmes and that closer working with local groups would improve this.

'We aren't paid employees or elected representatives and therefore don't have a place in the system. So if you're trying to do anything constructive in the community, but you're not part of that formal process, you don't fit.'

'Planning is set up as an adversarial process. What we've got is a development system that's not geared to collaborating, it's a system that's forever having to defend itself and react.'

'We need a recognition that there's a huge amount of valuable stuff in the community and it can be brought into the system. We need a shift in the top-down system to understand and interact with the community information system that is evolving with great potential.'

'It's a major flaw in consultation that there are all these community organisations which bring all this knowledge together but the process prevents them from communicating with each other. It only allows this vertical hierarchical communication, so the architects are just getting information out of you. You need a process that allows and encourages people to share ideas with each other. People can make a much more useful contribution in getting their views across if they've had a chance to check them out with other local people who know the place they're talking about.'

'To really involve local people, you need to go to where they will be, the everyday places that people use, like supermarkets, for instance. You have to use local know-how to identify the best ways to reach the public, and for that you need to talk to local people because they know what works and what doesn't.'

'It's a good idea for the architects to talk to the public groups from the outset, and see who can help in different areas. For public projects, they need to do more to spread the word and ask for volunteers from the community – would anyone like to help the architects reach out and connect and come up with ideas? It's good to have people on board who are involved with the community and have a heart for the community, and can help get people involved. I don't know if they just don't realise how much it would help, or if they're just wary that some groups will have too much control, but it means the architects have a lot more legwork to do.'

'There should have been publicity around the site itself, like big posters about the proposals, with a link to the planning website, so that everyone, whether visitors, residents, shoppers or shop-owners, could comment, instead of just getting the views of the few people that went to the workshops.'

'We ask architects, "What are you going to do to interest the public in the consultation?" to get them publicise it properly, because there's no point doing it if people don't know about it. And it helps them, because then there's less chance of lots of objections.'

'Some developers and their architects are quite good and will hire a hall and put boards up showing the plans, and have people there to answer questions, and that seems suitable for most developments. But it's no good hiring a hall and not telling anyone about the exhibition, and I think sometimes they then might try to pull the wool over the local authority's eyes and say, "Well we've had an exhibition, we've done our consultation."'

'The lead architect made a very telling comment at one meeting. Someone said something about the absence of local traders taking part in the process, and he said, "Well, we did invite them." But something special needed to be done for them. Many of the traders who operate the shops on the site don't have English as their first language, and work from morning till night.'

'Architects can't know everything about what the local situation is when they're planning a new development, but local people do, they know about site conditions and the locality and how things are there. Architects don't always look at the site in the wider context but local groups can, they have that experience of the area as a whole. It's a no-brainer, getting local people on your side, isn't it?'

'Developers are asked to talk to the planning groups here first before engaging with the public. We have people who can read drawings and who understand the development process and all the factors, and can talk to developers and architects on a more equal level. We can look at the plans together and work on them to produce something suitable together, and then we draw up a programme for community involvement, because we know how people will engage and how to approach it.'

10.4	METHODS AND EVENTS

What consultation methods and participation activities work? They all do, used at the right time in the right way. The comments in this section tend to focus on the things that could have been done better: making programmes less onerous; having knowledgeable staff available to answer questions; getting a good cross-section of the community involved; having a clear purpose to activities; providing meaningful information to enable people to make informed choices; using a mix of digital and in-person approaches and facilitating discussion amongst participants. Again there's a clear message that starting engagement early when options are open is seen as essential.

'There was a public exhibition, and the architects put their boards up to check out what people thought about the preferred option. The place was packed because it had stimulated people's interest. But then that was it, there was no process for further discussion together.'

'We discourage exhibitions at an early stage because showing plans then says that developers and designers have already made a lot of decisions. That's why we say there have to be discussions on the concept first, looking at the site and how the space could work. So go and talk to people about these things first, before deciding what it's going to look like.'

'Exhibitions are often held just before the planning application goes in and are done more as a courtesy than anything. It lets local groups get their act together before the consultation period, but that's not engagement.'

'Showing us some plans is not the same as asking us what we want.'

'The architects finally displayed a model of the proposals, which was sadly in an obscure location for just a couple of days, in a disused shop. There was nothing to inform people about it. And then that was it, it went in for planning.'

'The space on the site that was used to publicise the process was a good noticeable location and the architects put tables out and invited people in with tea and cake and that did attract interest.'

'There was a website where you could go in and put a flag with a comment on, but there was no way of having an exchange with anyone, or a conversation, and I think the reliance on that website spoiled the chances during that consultation period of us really airing the issues. We had no means for anyone who wanted to talk about these wider issues or share their views to do so.'

'We wanted something like a web forum, or a weekly drop-in, or a monthly meeting, something like that, for people to discuss with each other, to share thoughts and ideas.'

'There are some parts of the community that don't engage by coming to meetings and so on, but they want to be involved and have their say. Local groups on the ground know how best to engage with them, who to contact and what sort of approaches work best. But you do have to go to them, and this takes time. It's about early involvement again, you need to find out who to engage with early on, and identify the best ways of communicating with those groups.'

'Some groups definitely prefer interacting online and really get involved. But it doesn't work for all groups, and there are areas where a lot of people just aren't online and don't have computers at home, so engagement has to be face to face, and you have to attend meetings and listen to what people have to say.'

'There have been some Enquiry by Design programmes, which seem to work for big schemes and get better numbers involved. For individual buildings, we recommend talking to smaller numbers of people earlier rather than running these kinds of workshops. The reason is, we advocate making the process a conversation but it's more difficult to continue a conversation after those kinds of events. So when the design's been worked up a bit more after some discussion, the architects can come back and say which points have been incorporated and which haven't and the reasons, and we can continue a dialogue and work on the design until it reaches a stage when it can go in an exhibition for the public.'

'There were these indigestible workshops, where the architect would give lengthy Powerpoint presentations in enormous detail. There was no way that most of the people who weren't professionals in that world could digest it usefully. And then we'd have just half an hour for interaction with each other.'

'The workshops were basically presentations with too much technical detail and hardly any time for questions. Actually, we felt that was deliberate. The workshops weren't properly managed, we were just talked at, with no time for any interaction, no discussion of design options.'

'There were no models at the workshops, no sketches, nothing for us to interact with. It's like they didn't want interference in their design. They could have just had a whiteboard and done some quick sketch ideas so people could give their reactions, and then work up the agreed ideas using models and drawings that people could engage with, incorporating a consensus of community vision into a coherent design. But they gave us no options to discuss.'

'The people that came along to the workshops, well let's say it could have been more diverse. So I volunteered to set up a little stall at the leisure centre. I know loads of different people from going there every week, but it was just one kind of demographic getting involved in the consultation and loads of residents had no clue about the project.'

'The city decided to run a tenants' participation project about an extension to an estate that was something of a problem area. They appointed two architects who were rather inexperienced in participatory projects to work with the tenants' group, and it was hopeless because the architects just didn't know how to deal with these kinds of groups. It really needed a facilitator, so they brought one in and that made the project work. He could deal with tensions in the group, direct the discussion, and get things moving.'

'Participative events are more likely to be effective when efforts are made to ensure that all sorts of people can get involved. If you have a meeting, it's difficult for people with young children to come, or people who are at work will miss it and so on, and people get left out.'

'Sometimes planning authorities will use a shop for information about a proposal and people come and stare at models, which may or may not make sense to them. If there's nobody on hand to discuss it with or to answer questions it's a bit meaningless.'

'People felt enthusiastic about getting involved at the beginning but a year later they started to lose interest and there was less attendance at meetings and a loss of momentum. If the meetings and workshops had been better managed, people wouldn't have become disinterested, and if some of the architects hadn't bored the audience with superfluous technical material.'

10.5	**DECISION-MAKING AND OUTCOMES**

What influence do local people have on final decisions about space and design? To what extent are their wishes and needs reflected in the final proposal? It's clear that proposals that don't incorporate the public views expressed during an engagement programme leave lingering disillusionment.

'The final proposal involved totally redeveloping the whole site, even though we'd been told this was definitely not what was planned. We were baffled by the contradiction.'

'I think the only nod to the response from the public was lowering the heights of the buildings. They listened to public opinion in that we didn't want high-rise.'

'It was very much the architects' design in the end, and very corporate. It was imposed on us and doesn't reflect the community at all. It's a Corten steel theme park. There were a lot more objections to the planning application than support, but the council said it will go ahead anyway, so you're left wondering "What on earth was the point of all that?" After all this time, it was all just a big lip-service exercise, ticking the boxes. A complete waste of time and effort, and resources.'

'We were under the impression that the co-design process would gather information and then use that to start producing options for people to comment on, and work together towards a design. And that then there would still be a public consultation on the proposals as usual so that everyone could comment. What we didn't realise was that co-design was being used as a substitute for a consultation process. We weren't told it would go straight to planning.'

'Discussion about the public realm needs to involve a wide community of interests. The quality of public realm has such a wide impact, not just for the people in the immediate vicinity but on public space generally. We need to improve the quality of life in the public realm. If we lose the public realm, we lose a lot of the fundamental qualities of living in a particular place.'

'I assumed that designing a community space would involve the community. To most people a community space should be something that reflects its context and local community, not some narcissistic imposition. And something that could change with the community, not cast in stone and in steel, but something that could evolve. It should have been about expressing individuality and diversity.'

'Advice to designers: bear in mind the wider environment, the public realm and the streetscape. Look at where the development will sit, and how that has developed, and how the proposal will integrate. Developers need to recognise how the town has got to where it is now and go along with that.'

'The architects just went and did their own thing. They totally ignored all the feedback on what people wanted, which was a simple flexible space, a true community scheme with local artists', schools', residents' and shopkeepers' input, some trees, good lighting, cycle racks, places to sit, space for pop-ups, better transport interchange, public space. And to have a say in the choice of appropriate elements and materials, which was denied.'

'One problem I had with the workshops was that there was no discussion of the practicalities of anything, so for instance was the space going to be closed at night, or how the space would be managed, or security or protection, or whether the features were really practical.'

'Being clear about what all the options are from the start makes a difference, for instance making sure people understand that keeping X will mean losing Y, and budget factors, etc. But if this is explained, people will be quite reasonable usually.'

'We've had some cases that involved identifying problematic issues early on and working with the architects to design them out, which meant that local groups then actually supported those proposals and they've sailed through planning committee which might not have been the case otherwise. It shows how important early involvement is, and being flexible about the options. And it seems a better way than just chucking in a planning application and waiting to see what happens.'

10.6	PERCEPTIONS OF PROFESSIONALS

There's a recognition that the role of the designer in satisfying the client, the public and the planning committee, within time, budget and site constraints, isn't an easy one. Some of the architects involved clearly wanted to do the best they could in design and engagement terms. The theme of professional aloofness recurs, however, indicating a perceived failure to appreciate the worth of what the community can bring to a project.

'I don't think architects see the value of community involvement, of bringing in people who aren't architects or other specialists. The first duty is to satisfy the employer and their contracts. Where does the public fit into that? There's no space at all.'

'Architects are more interested in buildings than people. That's what they're really focused on.'

'They were very patronising. Of course we know there are technical constraints – actually several residents were architects and designers themselves so were totally prepared to be flexible, but we felt the architects were being incredibly opaque.'

'Real engagement has to be done in a real way. Designers have to come out and talk to people.'

'If architects want to understand what the general public think, they have to get involved to find out. And there are so many life issues bound up with it all. There are architects with the best intentions, but they have to get people involved.'

'I think some architects try their best, in a very defective system. But unfortunately some don't have a clue.'

'The architects didn't seem to want to collaborate, I think because they felt it was taking away their design powers. It was obvious they didn't want local community design input from the way they held us at arm's length.'

'Many architects don't understand what people value in places. When people talk about what's important to them, it tends to be stuff that most architects wouldn't notice, about the life of the place, so you have to get designers to understand that sort of thing.'

'Consultations should aim to improve on the original idea. I can understand designers being annoyed by having to make changes to their plans, so it would be better if they understood what people wanted from the outset, and then they could make changes to the proposal and not get upset.'

'We've sometimes ended up working together with architects when we've said for instance that we'd like to see more green space or better flood protection or more sustainability or whatever in their proposal, and they've said, "Great, can you please put that in writing to the developer because that's what we want too but they don't think it matters." So sometimes it's difficult for designers too, we know that.'

'Architects are getting better at communication. They aren't trained to think about it, or they certainly never used to be. It's all about design and nothing about listening to people or looking at the wider picture. As an architect, you tend to look at the site and the buildings around it, but not the neighbourhood as such. But what architects do affects a neighbourhood, and they need to understand that neighbourhood. They need to look at the bigger picture.'

'One architect said to me "I didn't do seven years of training just to be told what to do by people who know nothing about design."'

10.7	PROCESS

What makes a good engagement process? There were views across the spectrum, from a radical re-think of development planning system and its relationship to the local community, to giving local people more say in deciding the process they want, and greater transparency by developers. Early involvement with the community was a recurring theme: there was a strong feeling that engaging as soon as possible would benefit everyone involved.

'We should be thinking about a paradigm shift, a total break, not more-of-the-same-but-better, but something completely different. Real co-production needs to grasp that the community base that we're trying to bring into the process is actually a very different kind of system, and unless very different things start to happen, it will unfortunately just have the same problems and consequences that we've always had. But it could be different and real, it could be transformative.'

'Developers are getting more sympathetic to involving the public. It used to be a formal process so they would draw up their plans and present them and it was basically like it or lump it. But the environment is higher up peoples' agendas now and developers want to be seen supporting that sort of cause. There's more concern on the part of developers to provide something that's appreciated.'

'It's essential that there's an agreed process that the community decides for itself about how it shares its ideas and holds discussions throughout the whole thing.'

'There has to be an advantage in doing things another way and creating real community involvement. The big advantage to developers is improving certainty, so they know what local conditions they're facing, and understand what the local concerns are before the application goes in.'

'The ramifications of a bad process are that things then have to be done to correct and mitigate the effects of previous errors. Which is costly and wasteful.'

'Real co-design cannot happen unless there's full collaboration on the remit before it gets set in stone. How can you have a co-design process if you don't co-design the brief?'

'They talk about managing public expectations but it should be about developing expectations together. Agreeing a process together, not damping down public enthusiasm.'

'Even though the whole point is to build community trust and ensure a smooth ride through planning, some parties, including developers and architects, still seem to act as though they don't want anyone to know about the proposal. They seem to patronise the public, and just pay lip service and tick their boxes, and involve as few people as possible.'

'Our civic society encourages developers to talk to us long before they make an application, and we suggested that the local authority ask them to do this as well, which they do and this helps a lot. It's much easier for them to make changes at the pre-application stage if we discuss it together rather than once it's been formalised and is out for consultation.'

'If the developer says, "We're prepared to listen to your requirements and meet them when we can", then it shows a willingness to listen. They realise that they need to get the public on side and market the consultation properly, and explain their intentions, with an attitude of "We want to work with you so the finished result is one we can all be proud of."'

'The community and the local authority worked together to produce a Statement of Community Involvement Ground Rules, which is a good practice guide for developers on planning proposals. One of the important ground rules is for developers to start discussions while options for the development are still open, and it requires being very open about the options and about what choices are available. The original reaction amongst developers and designers was horror, but it's accepted now. They've seen that early involvement with the community brings greater certainty to projects, in terms of costs and how long they'll take to complete, if there are fewer objections because things have been agreed from the start.'

'By talking to local groups earlier, and in a negotiating way, developers can get support for a proposal if the local community gets something in return or the scheme creates other benefits. So there are positives for everyone if local people get something they want as well.'

'Early involvement is the biggest thing that architects need to deal with. They seldom come in at the early stages, but they need to approach local communities right from the start. And they need to promote the opportunities and benefits the community can get from the development, and not just think about their own interests.'

10.8	CONCLUSION

I offer these words from participants in the hope that the easily avoidable issues they highlight – about early involvement, valuing local expertise, openness and listening – are taken on board, because they are so easily remedied, but can cause real problems if ignored. The theme of this book is gathering good information in order to make good decisions and develop good designs. I hope this chapter serves as reminder of the human context of development and the value of community participation.

Bias

'Bias' in a research context denotes any kind of skew that affects how data is collected, analysed or communicated, and impacts on its accuracy.

- **Researcher bias** is when a researcher's preconceptions may lead them to misinterpret or misrepresent data. This also includes methodological bias, which refers to aspects of the research process itself that could affect the data collection or analysis.
- **Participant bias** is the influence of factors on participants that consciously or unconsciously affects their responses, such that they may not be a true reflection of their values or behaviour.

Data

The term 'data' is used loosely in this book to cover the products of any activity undertaken in pursuit of the research objectives. Data is the raw material generated by research: survey results, notes of discussions, photos, models, drawings, diaries, maps and observation results, and so on. The information derived from this raw material is also described as data.

Data library

A central project resource where all research data is stored, with an indexing or cataloguing system for search and retrieval.

Ethics

Ethical practice is all about the rights and responsibilities of researchers and participants (or designers and communities in the present context). Social research practice is founded on an ethical basis of integrity, transparency and impartiality, with obligations to safeguard participants and those conducting the research, to treat participants with respect and dignity, and to maintain high standards of integrity and professionalism throughout the project.

'Hard to reach' groups

This book refers to 'marginalised' instead of 'hard to reach' groups, in order to highlight the ethical responsibility for including and serving these communities rather than implying a failure to participate on their part. Examples, but not an exhaustive list, of groups who may be marginalised with particular regard to the urban environment and engagement processes include (in no particular order): people with mobility, cognitive or sensory impairments; people with chronic health problems or physical disabilities; young people; older people; LGBT people; ethnic or cultural minorities; refugees and asylum seekers; people with learning disabilities; people with mental health problems; homeless people; travellers; people in insecure employment or housing; and people with low literacy.

Informed consent

A key element of ethical practice, which requires that people are provided with all the information they need to decide whether to participate in a project. This might include explaining any risks and the measures in place to minimise them; explaining what will be involved and how long it will all take; allowing enough time for people to make their decisions; and giving an opportunity to ask questions and to receive useful responses. It's especially important to gain informed consent from children and people with learning difficulties or cognitive impairments.

Operationalisation

Research objectives are operationalised when they are turned into more detailed areas of study that can be expressed as specific and actionable questions. For example, this might mean translating theoretical issues into practical terms or deciding how to quantify an abstract quality.

Placemaking

The Project for Public Spaces defines placemaking as 'A collaborative process by which we can shape our public realm in order to maximize shared value. More than just promoting better urban design, placemaking facilitates creative patterns of use, paying particular attention to the physical, cultural, and social identities that define a place and support its ongoing evolution' (PPS, 2016).

Qualitative data/methods

Qualitative research approaches are generally used to understand issues of 'why' and 'how' about a topic. They tend to use open-ended questions, in-depth discussions and images, which provides data that is rich but complex.

Quantitative data/methods

Quantitative research approaches generally use standardised, replicable methods of gathering data to offer insight into when, what, where and how many. Methods like surveys, counting and mapping generate numerical or location-based data to provide statistics, charts and tables.

Reliability

Reliability is one of the key components of good social research practice, as it guards against bias. It means that if a research study was to be replicated on the same population by another team, the results and findings would be much the same. This requires that data is collected and analysed impartially, as far as possible.

Research objectives

Research objectives derive from the research strategy and state the project's intended overall outcomes in its broadest terms, completing the sentence 'This research will ...'

Research questions

Research questions operationalise the research objectives into smaller specific researchable topics, expressed as answerable questions.

Research strategy

The research strategy defines a project's scope and rationale, providing guidance for the project's duration. It answers the questions of 'What do we need to know?', 'Who should we engage with to get the information we need?' and 'How should we gather that information?' The strategy also includes details of methodology, resourcing, timescales, outputs, roles and responsibilities, and other relevant project details.

Sampling

The process of selecting project participants from the entire pool of potential participants. This may be randomised, which aims to involve a representative cross-section of participants, or purposive, where participants from particular groups are required.

Social research

A field of study within the humanities that looks at the social worlds of human groups and societies, and social trends and processes.

Validity

Validity is about operationalising research objectives into effective questions, and deciding on valid ways to gather the information required. It's also about correctly interpreting data and applying it when there are conclusions to be drawn, findings to be reported and recommendations to be made, which must all be derived impartially from the data.

BIBLIOGRAPHY

Bliss, L. (2017) *The High Line's next balancing act* [Online]. Available at: https://www.citylab.com/solutions/2017/02/the-high-lines-next-balancing-act-fair-and-affordable-development/515391/

Blundell Jones, P., Petrescu, D. & Till, J. (eds) (2005) *Architecture and participation*. Abingdon: Routledge.

Department for Work and Pensions (2017) *Family resources survey 2015/16* [Online]. London: Department for Work and Pensions. Available at: https://www.gov.uk/government/uploads/system/uploads/attachment_data/file/600465/family-resources-survey-2015-16.pdf

Ellard, C. (2014) 'Cities and their psychology: how neuroscience affects urban planning,' *The Guardian*, 4 February [Online]. Available at: https://www.theguardian.com/cities/2014/feb/04/cities-psychology-neuroscience-urban-planning-study

Ermacora, T. and Bullivant, L. (2015) *Recoded city: co-creating urban futures*. Abingdon: Routledge.

Gehl, J. (2011) *Life between buildings: using public space*, 6th ed. Washington, DC: Island Press.

Gehl, J. and Svarre, B. (2013) *How to study public life*. Washington, DC: Island Press.

International Association for Public Participation (2014) *IAP2's public participation spectrum*. Louisville, CO: IAP2.
Available at: https://c.ymcdn.com/sites/www.iap2.org/resource/resmgr/foundations_course/IAP2_P2_Spectrum_FINAL.pdf

Jacobs, J. (1961) *The death and life of great American cities*. New York, NY: Vintage Books.

Kahneman, D. (2011) *Thinking, fast and slow*. London: Penguin.

Larsson, N. (2016) 'The app that gives Oslo's children a direct say over their own road safety.' *The Guardian*, 2 September [Online]. Available at: https://www.theguardian.com/public-leaders-network/2016/sep/02/app-oslo-children-traffic-road-safety

Market Research Society (2012) *MRS guidelines for research with children and young people* (updated September 2014) [Online]. London: MRS. Available at: https://www.mrs.org.uk/pdf/2014-09-01Children%20and%20Young%20People%20

Research%20Guidelines.pdf

Martin, B. and Hanington, B. (2012) *Universal methods of design: 100 ways to research complex problems, develop innovative ideas, and design effective solutions.* Beverly, MA: Rockport Publishers.

Muratovski, G. (2016) *Research for designers: a guide to methods and practice.* London: SAGE Publications.

Nielsen, J. (2012) *Usability 101: introduction to usability* [Online]. Available at: https://www.nngroup.com/articles/usability-101-introduction-to-usability/

Popper, K. (1959) *The logic of scientific discovery.* New York, NY: Basic Books.

Project for Public Spaces (2016) *Placemaking: what if we built our cities around places?* [Online]. Available at: http://www.pps.org/wp-content/uploads/2016/10/Oct-2016-placemaking-booklet.pdf

Sanoff, H. (2000) *Community participation methods in design and planning.* New York, NY: John Wiley.

Sharon, T. (2015) *It's our research: getting stakeholder buy-in for user experience research projects.*

Waltham, MA: Morgan Kaufmann.

Stewart, D, and Shamdasani, P. (2014) *Focus groups: theory and practice,* 3rd ed. London: SAGE Publications.

UK Research Integrity Office (2009) *Code of practice for research: promoting good practice and preventing misconduct* [Online]. London: UKRIO. Available at: http://ukrio.org/publications/code-of-practice-for-research/

Wates, N. (2014) *The community planning handbook: how people can shape their cities, towns and villages in any part of the world,* 2nd ed. Abingdon: Routledge.

Weinschenk, S. (2011) *100 things every designer needs to know about people.* Berkeley, CA: New Riders.

Whyte, W.H. (1980) *The social life of small urban spaces.* New York, NY: Conservation Foundation.

Bias refers to factors that can skew how research data is collected, analysed or communicated, and potentially impact on accuracy. This appendix lists some of the main types of bias that could affect the kind of research covered in this book. They fall into two categories:

- **Researcher bias,** which arises on the research team side in aspects of how a study is planned, implemented, analysed and reported.
- **Participant bias,** which refers to issues that participants bring to the process that affect their responses, whether decision-making, information-processing or group dynamics.

RESEARCHER BIAS

Planning

Exclusion bias | A sampling issue in which the omission of particular groups data skews the data, especially relevant to marginalised groups.

Non-response bias | A study can be biased if the people who didn't take part would have responded differently to those who did.

Sampling bias | A general sampling issue arising from decisions about who to involve in a participation programme. The data could be biased if certain groups are under- or over-represented, or if only participants from a narrow demographic range are involved.

Selection bias | A sampling issue in which some individuals or groups are more likely than others to be studied or invited to participate in a research project.

Self-selection bias | A self-selecting sample means that all participants decided themselves to participate. Bias occurs when factors that influenced that decision gives the sample some specific characteristics: for example, by appealing to particular groups or traits.

Data collection

Attrition bias | A sampling issue in which data is skewed by participants dropping out of a programme or not completing tasks. (In larger numbers this may indicate that the strategy or task needs to be reviewed.)

Interviewer bias | While gathering information from groups or individuals, a researcher may unconsciously give cues through body language, wording or tone of voice that influence how people respond. The researcher's questioning style or personal manner can also affect responses, positively or negatively.

Measurement bias | An error where the method in use doesn't accurately measure what it's intended to measure; for example, a flawed counting strategy in an observation study that gives unreliable results.

Observer bias | A researcher's presence can influence responses from groups or individuals, even the researcher only observes and doesn't take part.

Procedural bias | This refers to flawed data-gathering procedures that can bias the results; for example, allowing insufficient time to complete questionnaires, holding meetings in venues that aren't fully accessible, using online-only communications, and so on.

Question-order bias | In questionnaires, the language and concepts that a question uses can affect responses to subsequent questions, such that participants might have given different responses had the same questions been asked in a different order. Questionnaire structure and wording needs careful consideration to minimise this effect.

Analysis

Clustering illusion | Misattributing or overestimating the significance of patterns in data that are just random.

Confirmation bias | Researchers may unwittingly look for or focus on information that confirms their own preconceptions, or interpret data as supporting those preconceptions while discounting data that doesn't.

Culture bias | Researchers are products of their culture; their assumptions, values and beliefs are shaped by their cultural background. This bias can be managed but not eliminated, and it's particularly important to be aware of when working with diverse groups.

Focusing effect | Attaching disproportionate importance to a set of data, a particular group or an event, for instance, which then erroneously becomes a focal point.

Group attribution error | Researchers may make the mistake in data gathering and analysis of believing that one individual is representative or speaks for a whole group.

Illusory correlation | The perception that two unrelated factors appear to be connected, when they're not.

Observer-expectancy effect | As with confirmation bias, researchers may tend to focus on data that was expected, while overlooking that which wasn't, or avoiding data that could support different findings.

Stereotyping | Researchers may expect members of a group to have certain characteristics or values based on assumptions about that demographic, which biases their preconceptions during data gathering and analysis.

Communication

Curse of Knowledge | The difficulty that experts and those immersed in a subject have in remembering what it's like to know very little about it.

Reporting bias | Some types of data are more likely than others to be reported; data that's easier to analyse, summarise and communicate, or that offers clear-cut interpretation, for example. There can also be a bias towards data that supports a preferred outcome or shows desired results.

PARTICIPANT BIAS

Acquiescence bias | Participants may readily agree with any ideas or suggestions put to them, which can indicate boredom, fatigue or wanting to complete the task quickly. Re-framing questions can check the validity of responses.

Affect heuristic | Put crudely, an unconscious factor in decision-making whereby people believe that the things they like are good, and things they dislike are bad, so that they equate feelings with beliefs. This means that if people are asked what they think of X, they will often say how they feel about it.

Anchoring | People often rely on the first information they received about a subject, which then becomes a mental reference point that shapes decisions or preferences even when new information is available.

Availability cascade | A phenomenon when awareness of a relatively minor matter escalates, reinforced by widespread repetition, such that it becomes a major public concern.

Availability heuristic | If instances of things are recalled easily, it creates the impression they are more common, normal or frequent than they really are.

Base rate fallacy | The tendency to focus on specific details or individual cases and ignore general information.

Bikeshedding | In consultations, minor design issues can become the focus in preference to more consequential matters and the bigger picture. (The reference is to fixating on the design of a nuclear power station's bicycle shelter.)

Bizarreness effect | People tend to remember the strange and unexpected more than the commonplace.

Concept test bias | In UX focus groups, participants may respond differently to a prototype or concept test depending whether it's introduced at the start, in the middle or at the end of the session. (Introduction at the start gives the least biased responses, as nothing in the session has influenced participants yet.)

Consistency bias | Survey respondents may sometimes sacrifice truthfulness for the sake of consistency in their answers.

Dominant respondent bias | In groups, participants may be influenced by a dominant individual who may be particularly knowledgeable or charismatic, and consciously or unconsciously adopt their responses.

First speaker bias | The first response to a question or new discussion topic in a group can influence the rest of the group's responses either by setting the tone or agenda, or creating the unconscious impression that the first speaker has the most knowledge of the matter.

Framing effect | People may draw different conclusions from the same information when it's presented in a different way.

Habituation bias | Participants in groups or survey respondents may give similar answers to questions that are worded in a similar way or that feel repetitive.

Halo effect | When people receive a favourable impression of an aspect of something (or someone), people may then create a 'halo' by attributing other positive characteristics or believing in other positive qualities, without experiencing them.

Hostility bias | People in groups may give extra-negative responses if they feel antipathy towards someone or something involved in the discussion; this could be a facilitator, other members, the developer, the designers, the proposals, the process, the venue or any other aspect.

Illusory truth effect | If a statement is easily processed, and/or is made repeatedly, people can be more likely to believe it to be true.

Ingroup bias | People tend to give preferential treatment to those they perceive to be members of their own groups.

Moderator acceptance bias | Participants in groups may give responses intended to please the facilitator or put themselves in a favourable light.

Overstatement bias | People may state their opinions more forcefully and simplistically in group discussions, so that participants' responses may appear more definitive than they were.

Reactive devaluation | People will sometimes disparage others' comments based on a dislike of the person who made them, or a group they're felt to represent, rather than the substance of what they said.

Recall bias | Participants may not remember past events accurately or completely, and may over- or underestimate their significance as a result.

Serial position effect | In processing any kind of information, people recall the items at the beginning and end of a sequence more easily; those in the middle are the most likely to be forgotten.

Shared information bias | People in group situations tend to spend more time and energy discussing information that's familiar to all members, and less on matters that only some members are aware of.

Social desirability effect | Participants may give what they think is the 'correct' answer, or one which reflects favourably on them, rather than disclose less socially acceptable behaviour or attitudes.

Sponsorship bias | Survey respondents and focus group participants may answer questions differently depending on who they perceive to be asking the questions.

Vividness effect | People tend to remember and be more affected by highly emotionally charged information and images, which can skew their recall and shape opinions and feelings disproportionately.

INDEX